The little PASTA cookbook

The little PASTA cookbook

MURDOCH BOOKS
SYDNEY · LONDON

Contents

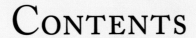

THE ITALIAN WORD 'PASTA' JUST MEANS 'PASTE' BUT 'PASTE' HARDLY DOES JUSTICE TO THE ASTONISHING DIVERSITY OF PASTA.

We have finally discovered a cookery secret the Italians have known for centuries: it is difficult to go wrong with pasta. What could be simpler or more appealing than butter and shavings of parmesan melting over a bowl of fresh tagliatelle? As comfort food, pasta is unbeatable. It is warming, filling and, above all, mouthwateringly delicious.

It was said that Marco Polo brought pasta to Italy from China in 1295, a rumour that does great disservice to the ancient Italians, who had been tucking in to pasta since the days of Imperial Rome. Cicero himself, so legend has it, was inordinately fond of laganum, the flat, ribbon pasta we now call tagliatelle. And, from the middle ages, Tasso's story tells how an innkeeper invented tortellini in the image of Venus's navel. So, if you're enjoying your pasta, you're in good company.

There are good reasons why pasta is such a popular food: it's cheap, it's quick and easy to prepare, it's delicious, it's nutritious and, as this book demonstrates, it's amazingly versatile. You can dress up pasta for a dinner party with a creamy smoked salmon sauce, or serve it simply, with parmesan or bacon and eggs. You can serve it cold in salads, warm in soups or piping hot from the oven, stuffed with spinach and ricotta. You can serve it for dessert and you can even serve it as a hangover cure—according to Italians, spaghetti with garlic and chilli oil, eaten before going to sleep, will ward off the after effects of too much vino. You can eat pasta every day of the week (as indeed many Italians do) and never tire of it. Pasta goes well with anything, including breads, vegetables and salads, which is why we have included ideas for these throughout the book.

And of course, there is the traditional accompaniment to some pasta dishes, parmesan. Although small amounts of grated parmesan, or little shavings, do look attractive, resist the temptation to serve it with everything. Avoid it with seafood sauces, in particular, as the flavours do not always mix well.

DRIED OR FRESH

Many people think that fresh pasta must be better than dried. This is not always the case— some sauces are better teamed with fresh pasta and some are best with dried. Fresh pasta works well with rich sauces made from cream, butter and cheese, because its soft texture absorbs the sauce. Alfredo is one of the nicest sauces to serve on fresh home-made pasta, as is a simple topping of butter and grated parmesan. Dried pasta is the one to choose if you're serving a heartier, tomato-based sauce. If your sauce has olives, anchovies, chilli, meat or seafood, you'll almost certainly need dried.

Pasta is a combination of flour, water and sometimes eggs and oil. Pasta made with wholewheat flour is darker. If dried pasta is made with durum wheat flour, it is considered to be of superior quality. Other dried pastas that are available include those made from different flours and cereals such as buckwheat, corn, rice and soya beans. Pastas are sometimes flavoured with a purée of herbs, tomato, spinach or other vegetables. Dried pasta will last up to six months, stored in an airtight container in a cool, dark place. However, dried wholewheat pasta will only last for one month before turning rancid. Fresh pasta can be wrapped in plastic and frozen for five days. If double wrapped, it will last up to four months. Don't thaw before cooking.

WHICH PASTA SHAPE?

There are good reasons for matching one pasta shape with a particular sauce. Apart from the traditional regional preference for a local shape, its ability to hold and support the sauce is all important. Tubular shapes such as penne capture thick sauces, while flat or long pastas are traditionally served with thin, smooth sauces. But there are no hard and fast rules and part of the fun of pasta is trying out all those fabulous colours, flavours and shapes. In this book you'll find photographs of some of the many fresh and dried pastas now available.

A lot of information about the pasta contained in the packet can be gleaned from its name. A name ending in -ricce means the pasta has a wavy edge; -nidi indicates that the lengths are formed into nests; -rigate means ridged and -lisce, smooth surfaced. And, if your Italian is up to scratch, you can pretty much visualise your pasta from its name ... although sometimes you may find this a little offputting. If the name of the pasta ends

with -oni, this indicates a larger size: for example, conchiglioni are large conchiglie. Likewise, -ini and -ette means smaller versions, as in farfallini. However, before we become too embroiled in the importance of names, let us point out that they do vary from manufacturer to manufacturer and book to book ... one man's tortelloni can be another man's agnolotti. Luckily, if a little commonsense is used, this isn't going to pose problems of life-threatening importance.

HOW MUCH PASTA?

Another highly charged subject as far as pasta aficionados are concerned, is how much pasta each person should be served and, even more controversially, how much sauce should be served on that pasta. As a general guide, use 60 g (2 oz) of fresh pasta per person for a starter, and 125 g (4 oz) for a main dish. You should allow a little bit more if you are using dried (it contains less moisture, so is lighter), about 90 g (3 oz) each for a starter and 150 g (5 oz) per person for a main dish.

How much sauce is obviously a matter of personal taste, but the biggest mistake non-Italian cooks make is to use too much sauce: the pasta should be lightly coated, not drenched. When the pasta and sauce are tossed, there shouldn't be extra sauce swimming around at the bottom.

COOKING YOUR PASTA

Unsalted water will come to the boil faster than salted water, so add the salt once the water is boiling. Use a large pan of water, enough so that the pasta has plenty of room to move around, and only add the pasta when the water has reached a rapid boil. Some people like to add a tablespoon of olive oil to help prevent the water boiling over or the pasta sticking together. After the pasta has been added, cover the pan to help bring the water back to the boil as quickly as possible, then remove the lid as soon as the water returns to the boil. Al dente ('to the bite') is how Italians describe the texture of well-cooked pasta. Test pasta towards the end of cooking; it should feel slightly elastic

and you should feel a little resistance as you bite the pasta (or break it using your thumb); however, it should not be at all chalky in the centre.

Timing is the difference between a good pasta meal and a great one. Read the recipe through first and coordinate your cooking times. Have the table set, parmesan cheese (if using) grated and the serving bowls warmed. Aim to have the sauce ready to dress the pasta as soon as it is cooked, especially for fresh pasta, which will continue to cook slightly, even once drained.

It is important to add the pasta to the sauce after draining. Don't overdrain the pasta or shake it too vigorously in the colander—it needs to be slippery for the sauce to coat it well. Never leave cooked pasta sitting in the colander for long—fresh pasta, especially, can become a sticky mass.

The only times you might rinse pasta is if you are going to serve it cold, or when blanching fresh sheets for lasagne. Rinse it under cold water or place in a bowl of iced water to arrest the cooking, then drain and toss it in a little oil to prevent it from sticking together. Cover and refrigerate if not using immediately.

Chapter 1

CLASSIC SAUCES

Sometimes it's difficult to determine whether you're eating pasta with your sauce or sauce with your pasta. While the difference is subtle, the Italians intended their pasta to be evenly dressed by its sauce, rather than swimming in it. Prepare these classic sauces using the freshest ingredients and toss them through a bowl of pasta.

SPAGHETTI ALLE VONGOLE

Spaghetti with Clams

This traditional Neapolitan dish is especially popular throughout central Italy. The addition of tomatoes (*in rosso*) is less common in the south of the country where the dish is traditionally served without them (*in blanco*).

1 kg (2 lb 4 oz) small fresh clams (vongole) in shells, cleaned (see note) or 750 g (1 lb 10 oz) tinned clams in brine
1 tablespoon lemon juice
4 tablespoons olive oil

3 garlic cloves, crushed
850 g (1 lb 14 oz) tinned chopped tomatoes
250 g (9 oz) spaghetti
4 tablespoons chopped parsley

Place the cleaned clams in a large saucepan with the lemon juice. Cover the pan tightly and shake over medium heat for 7–8 minutes until the shells open (discard any clams that do not open in this time). Remove the clams from their shells. If using tinned clams, rinse well, drain and set aside.

Heat the oil in a large saucepan. Add the garlic and cook over low heat for 5 minutes. Add the tomatoes and stir well. Bring to the boil and simmer, covered, for 20 minutes. Add the clams to the sauce and season with freshly ground black pepper. Stir until heated through.

Meanwhile, cook the pasta in a large saucepan of rapidly boiling salted water until al dente. Drain well and return to the pan. Add the sauce and chopped parsley and toss gently.

Note: To clean the clams, any sand and grit needs to be drawn out of the shells. Combine 2 tablespoons each of salt and plain flour with enough water to make a paste. Add to a large bucket or bowl of cold water and soak the clams in this mixture overnight. Drain and scrub the shells well, then rinse thoroughly and drain again.

SERVES 4

Add the clam sauce and the parsley to the warm pasta in the saucepan and toss gently.

PASTA AL GORGONZOLA

Pasta with Gorgonzola Sauce

This delicious sauce takes less than ten minutes to prepare and no more than fifteen minutes to cook. Gorgonzola is a rich, strong Italian blue-veined cheese

375 g (13 oz) spaghetti or bucatini
200 g (7 oz) gorgonzola cheese
250 g (9 oz/1 cup) fresh ricotta cheese

1 tablespoon salted butter
1 celery stalk, finely chopped
300 ml (10½ fl oz) pouring (whipping) cream

Cook the pasta in a large saucepan of rapidly boiling salted water until al dente. Drain well and return to the pan to keep warm. Meanwhile, chop the gorgonzola into small cubes and beat the ricotta until it is smooth.

Heat the butter in a frying pan, add the celery and stir for 2 minutes. Add the cream, ricotta and gorgonzola and season to taste.

Bring to the boil over low heat, stirring constantly. Reduce the heat and simmer for 1 minute. Toss well with the pasta.

SERVES 4–6

Far left: While the pasta is cooking, chop the gorgonzola cheese into cubes.

Left: Bring the sauce to the boil over low heat, stirring constantly to thicken it.

Pasta con Ragù alla Bolognese

Pasta Bolognese

Traditionally, bolognese is served with tagliatelle, but you can also use tube or ribbon shaped pasta as an alternative.

50 g (1¾ oz) salted butter
180 g (6¼ oz) thick bacon slices or speck, finely chopped
1 large onion, finely chopped
1 carrot, finely chopped
1 celery stalk, finely chopped
400 g (14 oz) lean minced (ground) beef

670 ml (23 fl oz/2⅔ cups) beef stock
250 g (9 oz) tinned chopped tomatoes
125 ml (4 fl oz/½ cup) dry red wine
¼ teaspoon freshly grated nutmeg
500 g (1 lb 2 oz) pasta
grated parmesan cheese, for serving

Heat half the butter in a heavy-based frying pan. Add the bacon and cook until golden. Add the onion, carrot and celery and cook over low heat for 8 minutes, stirring often.

Increase the heat, add the remaining butter and, when the pan is hot, add the beef. Break up any lumps with a wooden spoon and stir until brown. Add the beef stock, tomato, wine, nutmeg and season to taste.

Bring to the boil and then reduce the heat and simmer, covered, over very low heat for 2–5 hours, adding more stock if the sauce becomes too dry. The longer the sauce is cooked, the more flavour it will have.

Cook the pasta in a large saucepan of rapidly boiling salted water until al dente. Drain well and serve with the sauce and freshly grated parmesan cheese.

SERVES 4

Right: Finely chop the thick bacon slices or speck, after removing any rind.

Far right: Use the finest cutting side of the grater for the whole nutmeg.

Pasta Primavera

Spring Pasta

A combination of pasta and fresh spring vegetables. You can use other vegetables such as broccoli or carrots instead of the beans or peas. This dish is typically served with smaller pasta shapes such as penne.

500 g (1 lb 2 oz) pasta
155 g (5½ oz/1 cup) frozen broad (fava) beans
200 g (7 oz) sugar snap peas
150 g (5½ oz) asparagus spears

30 g (1 oz) salted butter
250 ml (9 fl oz/1 cup) pouring (whipping) cream
60 g (2¼ oz) grated parmesan cheese

Cook the pasta in a large saucepan of rapidly boiling salted water until al dente. Drain well and return to the pan to keep warm.

Cook the beans in boiling water for 2 minutes, then refresh in iced water and drain. Remove the skins from the beans—you can usually just squeeze them out, otherwise carefully slit the skins first.

Trim the stalks from the peas and snap the tough woody ends from the asparagus spears. Cut the asparagus into short lengths.

Melt the butter in a frying pan. Add the vegetables, cream and parmesan cheese. Simmer gently for 3–4 minutes, or until the peas and asparagus are just tender. Season to taste. Pour the sauce over the warm pasta and toss gently. Serve immediately.

SERVES 4

Far left: If the broad beans will not slip out of their skins easily, gently slit or break the ends first.

Left: Trim the stalks from the sugar snap peas. Snap the woody ends from the asparagus.

DRIED PASTA

Dried pasta is one of the main staples of the modern pantry. It's always on hand, quick and easy to prepare. Dried pasta is also sturdier than fresh and pairs with more flavour options than delicate-tasting fresh pasta.

Dried pasta is the one to choose for hearty tomato sauces. It has also traditionally been used to hold richer, oil-based sauces that contain olives, anchovies, meat or seafood, as it has a firmer, denser texture than fresh pasta when cooked. Flavours such as spinach and tomato may also be added to dried pasta. When shopping, it is worth spending a little extra money when buying dried pasta and getting a good-quality brand—inferior brands can have a disappointing texture.

Dried pasta is made with flour, water and sometimes eggs and oil. Dried pasta made with 100 per cent durum wheat flour (durum wheat is a variety with a higher gluten content) is considered to be of superior quality. Pasta made with wholemeal flour is darker and nuttier in flavour. Dried pastas can also be made with flour ground from other cereals, such as corn, buckwheat, rice and soya beans.

There are many shapes and sizes and a lot of information can be gleaned from the name of a type of pasta. A name ending in -ricce means the pasta has a wavy edge; rigate means ridged; and lisce means smooth surfaced. Some names are visual descriptions of the shape: orecchiette are little ears; eliche (a type of spiral pasta) are propellers; ditali (small short tubes) are thimbles; conchiglie are shells; linguine are little tongues; while vermicelli are little worms.

Dried long pasta can partner well with smooth tomato, creamy or oily sauces. Some of the wider long pastas can hold meat sauces too, as there is room for the sauce to nestle and cling to the pasta. Types include spaghetti, spaghettini, angel hair, linguine, fettuccine, pappardelle and reginette.

Dried shapes for baking are perfect for meat and vegetable pasta dishes—it's convenient to use dried pasta for these dishes as you can keep various types on hand at all times.

Some recipes call for them to be blanched before filling or layering. Types include lasagne sheets, cannelloni, conchiglioni and ziti.

Dried large shapes are great for chunky sauces as the dips and curves give the sauce something to cling to. Types include conchiglie, penne, rigatoni, pipe rigate, fusilli, orecchiette, rotelle and casarecci.

Dried small shapes are traditionally used with a simple sauce or as part of a soup. Children generally love small pasta shapes too. Types include macaroni, cavatelle, anelli, ditalini, stellini and risoni (also known as orzo).

pappardelle

fusilli or eliche

lumaconi or pipe rigate

macaroni or maccher

spaghetti

orecchiette

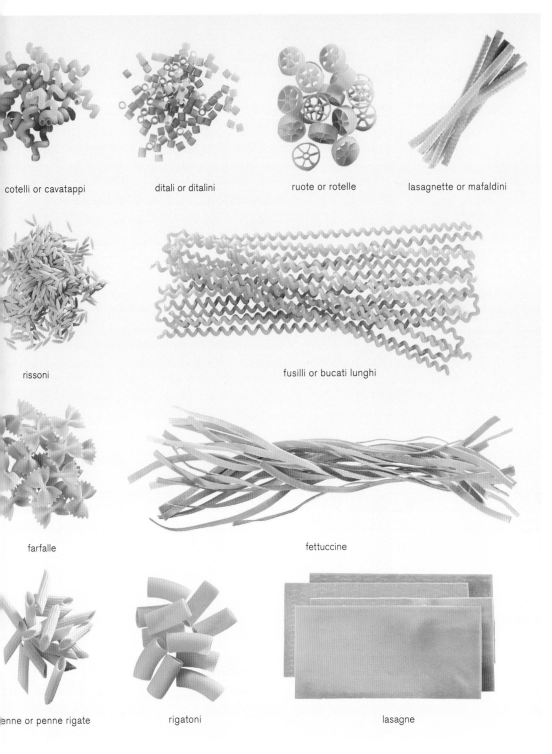

cotelli or cavatappi

ditali or ditalini

ruote or rotelle

lasagnette or mafaldini

rissoni

fusilli or bucati lunghi

farfalle

fettuccine

enne or penne rigate

rigatoni

lasagne

Pasta alla Boscaiola

Pasta Boscaiola

'Boscaiola' means woodcutter or lumberjack—collecting mushrooms is part of the woodcutter's heritage. This sauce is normally served with spaghetti, but you can use any pasta.

500 g (1 lb 2 oz) pasta
1 tablespoon olive oil
6 bacon slices, chopped
200 g (7 oz) button mushrooms, sliced

625 ml (21½ fl oz/2½ cups) pouring (whipping) cream
2 spring onions (scallions), sliced
1 tablespoon chopped parsley

Cook the pasta in a large saucepan of rapidly boiling salted water until al dente. Drain well and return to the pan to keep warm.

Meanwhile, heat the oil in a large frying pan, add the bacon and mushrooms and cook, stirring, for 5 minutes, or until golden brown.

Add a little of the cream and stir well with a wooden spoon.

Add the remaining cream, bring to the boil and cook over high heat for 15 minutes, or until thick enough to coat the back of a spoon. Add the spring onion. Pour the sauce over the pasta and toss well. Serve sprinkled with the parsley.

Note: If you are short on time and don't have 15 minutes to reduce the sauce, it can be thickened with 2 teaspoons of cornflour (cornstarch) mixed with 1 tablespoon of water. Stir until the mixture boils and thickens.

SERVES 4

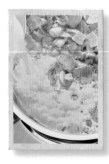

Far left: Add a little of the cream and scrape the bottom of the pan with a spoon.

Left: Cook the sauce over high heat until it is thick enough to coat the back of a spoon.

Pasta alla Marinara

Mariner's Pasta

Originally made without the addition of seafood, the high acidic content of the tomatoes, garlic and herbs, ensured the sauce remained edible for much longer than other sauces making it a popular choice on early sea voyages.

1 tablespoon olive oil
1 onion, chopped
2 garlic cloves, crushed
125 ml (4 fl oz/½ cup) dry red wine
2 tablespoons tomato paste (concentrated pureé)
425 g (15 oz) tinned chopped tomatoes
250 ml (9 fl oz/1 cup) bottled tomato pasta sauce
1 tablespoon chopped basil
1 tablespoon chopped oregano

12 mussels, scrubbed and beards removed (discard any which are open and don't close if tapped)
30 g (1 oz) salted butter
125 g (4½ oz) small squid tubes, sliced
125 g (4½ oz) boneless white fish fillets, cubed
200 g (7 oz) raw prawns (shrimp), peeled and deveined, tails intact
500 g (1 lb 2 oz) pasta

Heat the olive oil in a large saucepan. Add the onion and garlic and cook over low heat for 2–3 minutes. Increase the heat to medium and add the wine, tomato paste, tomato and pasta sauce. Simmer, stirring occasionally, for 5–10 minutes or until the sauce thickens slightly. Stir in the fresh herbs and season. Keep warm.

Heat 125 ml (4 fl oz/½ cup) water in a saucepan. Add the mussels, cover the pan tightly and steam for 3–5 minutes, or until the mussels have opened. Discard any that don't open in this time. Set the

mussels aside and stir the cooking liquid into the tomato sauce.

Heat the butter in a frying pan and sauté the squid, fish and prawns, in batches, for 1–2 minutes, or until cooked. Add the seafood, including the mussels, to the warm tomato sauce and stir gently.

Cook the pasta in a large saucepan of rapidly boiling salted water until al dente. Drain well and toss gently with the seafood sauce.

SERVES 4

Right: Scrub the mussels and pull away their beards. Discard any open mussels.

Far right: Remove the quills from inside the squid tubes and slice the tubes into thin rings.

PASTA AL PESTO
Pasta with Pesto

You can make the pesto up to one week before you need it. Traditionally, linguine is used with pesto but you can serve it with any pasta of your choice.

500 g (1 lb 2 oz) pasta
3 tablespoons pine nuts
2 very large handfuls basil leaves
2 garlic cloves, peeled

½ teaspoon salt
3 tablespoons grated parmesan cheese
2 tablespoons grated pecorino cheese, optional
125 ml (4 fl oz/½ cup) olive oil

Cook the pasta in a large saucepan of rapidly boiling salted water until al dente. Drain well and return to the pan to keep warm.

Meanwhile, toast the pine nuts in a dry heavy-based frying pan over low heat for 2–3 minutes, or until golden. Allow to cool. Process the pine nuts, basil leaves, garlic, salt and parmesan and pecorino (if using) cheeses in a food processor for 20 seconds, or until finely chopped.

With the motor running, gradually add the oil in a thin steady stream until a paste is formed. Add freshly ground black pepper, to taste.

Toss the sauce with the warm pasta until the pasta is well coated.

Note: Pesto sauce can be made up to 1 week in advance and refrigerated in an airtight container. Ensure the pesto is tightly packed and seal the surface with some plastic wrap or pour a little extra oil over the top to prevent the pesto turning black. Each time you use the pesto reseal the surface with a little oil.

SERVES 4–6

With the motor running, add the olive oil in a thin steady stream, until a paste is formed.

Pasta all'Amatriciana
Pasta Amatriciana

A traditional Italian pasta sauce based on cured pork. It is believed this dish originated in the town of Amatrice, where bacon is a prized local product.

6 thin slices pancetta or 3 bacon slices
1 kg (2 lb 4 oz) very ripe tomatoes (see notes)
500 g (1 lb 2 oz) pasta (see notes)
1 tablespoon olive oil

1 small onion, very finely chopped
2 teaspoons very finely chopped fresh chilli (see notes)
parmesan cheese shaved, for serving

Finely chop the pancetta or bacon. Score a cross in the base of each tomato. Soak in boiling water for 1 minute, then drain and plunge into cold water briefly. Peel the skin away from the cross. Halve the tomatoes, remove the seeds and chop the flesh.

Cook the pasta in a large saucepan of rapidly boiling salted water until al dente. Drain well and return to the pan to keep warm.

Meanwhile, heat the oil in a heavy-based frying pan. Add the pancetta or bacon, onion and chilli and stir over medium heat for 3 minutes. Add the tomato and season to taste. Reduce the heat and simmer for 3 minutes. Add the sauce to the pasta and toss until well combined. Serve garnished with shavings of parmesan cheese, if desired.

Notes: For a change from ordinary tomatoes, you can try roma (plum) tomatoes in this recipe. They are firm-fleshed with few seeds and have a rich flavour when cooked.

Traditionally, bucatini is served with this sauce, but you can use any pasta you prefer. It is shown here with penne.

To avoid skin irritation, wear rubber gloves when chopping or seeding chillies.

SERVES 4–6

Far left: Remove the tomatoes from the cold water and peel the skin down from the cross.

Left: Halve the tomatoes and scrape out the seeds with a teaspoon.

Pasta al Ragù

Pasta Ragù

If you want to serve this dish with a much creamier sauce you can add 185 ml (7 fl oz/¾ cup) pouring (whipping) cream just before serving.

180 g (6¼ oz) speck, or thick bacon slices
150 g (5½ oz) chicken livers
60 g (2¼ oz/¼ cup) salted butter
1 large onion, finely chopped
1 carrot, finely chopped
1 celery stalk, finely chopped
200 g (7 oz) minced (ground) veal

200 g (7 oz) minced (ground) pork
500 ml (17 fl oz/2 cups) beef stock
250 g (9 oz) tinned chopped tomatoes
125 ml (4 fl oz/½ cup) dry red wine
¼ teaspoon grated nutmeg
500 g (1 lb 2 oz) pasta
grated parmesan cheese, for serving

Chop the speck (or bacon) finely. Slice and finely chop the chicken livers. Heat about half the butter in a heavy-based frying pan. Add the speck and cook until golden brown. Add the onion, carrot and celery and cook over low heat for about 8 minutes, stirring occasionally.

Increase the heat, add the remaining butter and, when the pan is quite hot, add the veal and pork. Break up any lumps with a fork and stir until brown. Add the livers and cook, stirring, until they change colour. Add the stock, tomato, wine and nutmeg. Season, bring to the boil and simmer, covered, over very low heat for 2–5 hours, adding a little more stock if the sauce becomes too dry. The longer you cook the sauce the more flavour it will have.

Cook the pasta in a large saucepan of rapidly boiling salted water until al dente. Drain well and return to the pan. Add half the sauce and toss to combine. Serve the rest of the sauce over the top, with grated parmesan cheese.

SERVES 4–6

Right: Use a large sharp knife to finely chop the speck or bacon.

Far right: Break up any lumps of mince with a fork and stir until brown.

Pasta Napoletana

Pasta Napolitana

Napolitana sauce, also called Napoli sauce or Neapolitan sauce, is the collective name given (outside Italy) to various basic tomato-based sauces derived from Italian cuisine, often served over or with pasta.

2 tablespoons olive oil
1 onion, finely chopped
1 carrot, finely chopped
1 celery stalk, finely chopped
500 g (1 lb 2 oz) very ripe tomatoes, chopped

2 tablespoons chopped parsley
2 teaspoons sugar
500 g (1 lb 2 oz) pasta (see note)

Heat the oil in a heavy-based saucepan. Add the onion, carrot and celery. Cover and cook for 10 minutes over low heat, stirring occasionally.

Add the tomato to the pan with the parsley, sugar and 125 ml (4 fl oz/½ cup) water. Bring to the boil, reduce the heat to low, cover and simmer for 45 minutes, stirring occasionally. Season to taste. If necessary, add up to 185 ml (6 fl oz/¾ cup) more water if the sauce needs thinning.

Cook the pasta in a large saucepan of rapidly boiling salted water until al dente. Drain well and return to the pan. Toss gently with the sauce.

Notes: Traditionally, spaghetti is served with this sauce but we have shown fusilli. The sauce can be concentrated by cooking it for longer. Store in the refrigerator and add water or stock to thin it when reheating.

SERVES 4–6

Dice the tomatoes into small pieces, before adding with the parsley, sugar and water.

Pasta alla Puttanesca
Pasta Puttanesca

If you can't find tins of chopped tomatoes, use tinned whole tomatoes—simply chop the tomatoes in the tin with a pair of kitchen scissors.

500 g (1 lb 2 oz) spaghetti or fettuccine
2 tablespoons olive oil
3 garlic cloves, crushed
2 tablespoons chopped parsley
¼–½ teaspoon chilli flakes, or chilli powder

850 g (1 lb 14 oz) tinned chopped tomatoes
1 tablespoon capers, rinsed and drained
3 anchovy fillets, chopped
3 tablespoons black olives

Cook the spaghetti or fettuccine in a large saucepan of rapidly boiling salted water until al dente. Drain well and return to the pan to keep warm.

Meanwhile, heat the oil in a heavy-based frying pan. Add the garlic, parsley and chilli flakes and cook, stirring, for 1 minute over medium heat.

Add the tomato and stir to combine. Reduce the heat and simmer, covered, for 5 minutes.

Add the capers, anchovies and olives and cook, stirring, for 5 minutes. Season with freshly ground black pepper. Add the sauce to the pasta and toss together gently. Serve immediately.

SERVES 4–6

Gnocchi Spinaci e Ricotta
Spinach and Ricotta Gnocchi

The word gnocchi may derive from the Italian word nocchio, meaning a knot in wood, or from nocca (meaning knuckle).

4 slices white bread
125 ml (4 fl oz/½ cup) milk
500 g (1 lb 2 oz) frozen spinach, thawed
250 g (9 oz/1 cup) ricotta cheese
2 eggs
60 g (2¼ oz) grated parmesan cheese
30 g (1 oz/¼ cup) plain (all-purpose) flour

shaved parmesan cheese, for serving

GARLIC BUTTER SAUCE
100 g (3½ oz) salted butter
2 garlic cloves, crushed
3 tablespoons chopped basil
1 ripe tomato, diced

Remove the crusts from the bread and soak in milk in a shallow dish for 10 minutes. Squeeze out any excess milk from the bread. Squeeze out any excess liquid from the spinach.

Place the bread, spinach, ricotta, eggs and parmesan in a bowl and mix thoroughly. Refrigerate, covered, for 1 hour. Fold the flour in well.

Lightly dust your hands in flour and roll heaped teaspoons of the bread mixture into dumplings.

Lower batches of the gnocchi into a large saucepan of boiling salted water. Cook each batch for about 2 minutes, or until the gnocchi rise to the surface. Transfer to a serving plate and keep warm.

To make the sauce, combine all the ingredients in a small saucepan and cook over medium heat for 3 minutes, or until the butter is nutty brown. Drizzle over the gnocchi and sprinkle with the parmesan.

SERVES 4–6

Far left: Gently squeeze out any excess milk from the soaked bread.

Left: With floured hands, roll teaspoons of the mixture into dumplings.

Pasta all'Arrabbiata

Pasta Arrabbiata

'Arrabbiata' means 'angry' in Italian; the name of the sauce may well be a reference to the heat of the chilli pepper and its possible effect on unsuspecting diners.

75 g (2½ oz/½ cup) bacon fat
2–3 red chillies
2 tablespoons olive oil
1 large onion, finely chopped
1 garlic clove, finely chopped

500 g (1 lb 2 oz) very ripe tomatoes, finely chopped
500 g (1 lb 2 oz) pasta (see note)
2 tablespoons chopped parsley
grated parmesan cheese or pecorino cheese, for serving

Use a large knife to finely chop the bacon fat. Chop the chillies, taking care to avoid skin irritation—wearing rubber gloves will help. Heat the oil in a heavy-based frying pan and add the bacon fat, chilli, onion and garlic. Fry for 8 minutes, stirring occasionally.

Add the tomato to the pan with 125 ml (4 fl oz/½ cup) water and season to taste. Cover and simmer for about 40 minutes, or until the sauce is thick and rich.

When the sauce is almost cooked, cook the pasta in a large saucepan of rapidly boiling salted water until al dente. Drain well and return to the pan to keep warm.

Add the parsley to the sauce and toss gently through the pasta. Serve with the parmesan cheese or pecorino cheese sprinkled over the top, if desired.

Note: Penne rigate is traditionally served with this sauce. We have used pappardelle.

SERVES 4

Remove the stalks and slice the chillies in half. Wear rubber gloves to protect your skin.

Chapter 2

PASTA WITH MEAT

Beef, pork, lamb and many other meats are flavoured with herbs, and married with tomatoes, vegetables and wine to turn a straightforward bowl of pasta into a hearty, nutritious and truly delicious meal.

Pasta Mediterranea
Mediterranean Pasta

Fresh pasta tossed with herbs, nourishing vegetables and olive oil is a staple of the Mediterranean diet.

2 tablespoons olive oil
1 teaspoon dried oregano
2 garlic cloves, finely chopped
6 roma (plum) tomatoes, halved
500 g (1 lb 2 oz) spaghetti
4 slices prosciutto

16 kalamata olives
200 g (7 oz) feta cheese, cut into bite-sized cubes
1 tablespoon balsamic vinegar
100 ml (3½ fl oz) olive oil, extra
3 garlic cloves, thinly sliced, extra
60 g (2¼ oz) rocket (arugula) leaves

Preheat the oven to 150°C (300°F/Gas 2). Combine the olive oil, oregano, garlic and 1 teaspoon salt in a bowl. Add the tomato and toss to combine, rubbing the mixture onto the cut halves of the tomatoes. Place the tomato cut side up on a lined baking tray and cook in the oven for 1 hour.

Meanwhile, cook the pasta in a large saucepan of rapidly boiling salted water until al dente. Drain well and return to the pan to keep warm. Place the prosciutto on a grill tray and cook under a hot grill (broiler), turning once, for 3–4 minutes, or until crispy. Break into pieces.

Toss the tomato, olives, feta, spaghetti and balsamic vinegar in a bowl and keep warm.

Heat the extra olive oil in a small saucepan and cook the extra garlic over low heat, without burning, for 1–2 minutes, or until the garlic has infused the oil.

Pour the garlic and oil over the spaghetti mixture, add the rocket leaves and toss well. Sprinkle with the prosciutto pieces and season well. Serve immediately.

SERVES 4

Right: Rub the olive oil, oregano, garlic and salt mixture into the cut halves of the tomato.

Far right: Grill the prosciutto until crispy, then break into small pieces.

BUCATINI CON SALSICCIA E SEMI DI FINOCCHIO
Bucatini with Sausage and Fennel Seed

Bucatini resembles a thick spaghetti but with a hollow centre, known as the 'buco' or hole. This hole is perfect for retaining thick pasta sauces. Traditionally, bucatini was made by rolling pasta dough over a smooth stick to create the hollow centre.

500 g (1 lb 2 oz) Italian sausages
2 tablespoons olive oil
3 garlic cloves, chopped
1 teaspoon fennel seeds
½ teaspoon chilli flakes

850 g (1 lb 14 oz) tinned chopped tomatoes
500 g (1 lb 2 oz) bucatini
1 teaspoon balsamic vinegar
1 small handful basil, chopped

Heat a frying pan over high heat, add the sausages and cook, turning regularly, for 8–10 minutes, or until well browned and cooked through. Remove, cool slightly and slice thinly on the diagonal.

Heat the oil in a saucepan, add the garlic and cook over medium heat for 1 minute. Add the fennel seeds and chilli flakes and cook for a further minute. Stir in the tomato and bring to the boil, then reduce the heat and simmer, covered, for 20 minutes. Meanwhile, cook the pasta in a large saucepan of rapidly boiling salted water until al dente. Drain well and return to the pan to keep warm.

Add the sausages to the sauce and cook, uncovered, for 5 minutes to heat through. Stir in the balsamic vinegar and basil. Divide the pasta among four bowls, top with the sauce and serve.

SERVES 4

Far left: Fry the sausages until they are well browned then slice them on the diagonal.

Left: Cook the garlic, fennel seeds and chilli flakes in the oil.

Fusilli con Pancetta e Sugo di Fava

Fusilli with Bacon and Broad Bean Sauce

The broad beans form an essential part of this recipe and can be cooked and peeled in advance. Refrigerate in an airtight container until needed.

500 g (1 lb 2 oz) fusilli or penne
310 g (11 oz/2 cups) frozen broad (fava) beans
2 tablespoons olive oil
2 leeks, finely sliced

4 bacon slices, diced
310 ml (10¾ fl oz/1¼ cups) pouring (whipping) cream
2 teaspoons grated lemon zest

Cook the pasta in a large saucepan of rapidly boiling salted water until al dente. Drain well and return to the pan to keep warm. While the pasta is cooking, plunge the broad beans into a saucepan of boiling water. Remove with a slotted spoon and place immediately in cold water. Drain and allow to cool, then peel (see note).

Heat the oil in a heavy-based frying pan. Add the leek and bacon and cook over medium heat, stirring occasionally, for 8 minutes, or until the leek is golden. Add the cream and lemon zest and cook for 2 minutes. Add the broad beans and season well.

Add the sauce to the pasta and toss to combine. Serve at once.

Note: To peel the broad beans, break off the top and squeeze out the beans. Leaving the hard outside skin on the broad bean will change the delicate texture and flavour of this dish—it is worth the extra effort to peel them. Very young fresh broad beans can be used without peeling.

SERVES 4–6

Far left: Carefully remove the outer leaves and dark green section from the leeks. Clean them thoroughly.

Left: After cooling the broad beans, peel away the outer skins.

PENNE CON RAGÙ DI VITELLO

Penne with Veal Ragù

Most butchers sell veal shin cut into osso bucco pieces. If sold as a whole piece, ask your butcher to cut into pieces about 3–4 cm (1¼–1½ inches) thick.

2 onions, sliced
2 bay leaves, crushed
1.5 kg (3 lb 5 oz) veal shin, cut into osso bucco pieces
250 ml (9 fl oz/1 cup) dry red wine
800 g (1 lb 12 oz) tinned chopped tomatoes

375 m (13 fl oz/1½ cups) beef stock
2 teaspoons chopped rosemary
400 g (14 oz) penne
155 g (5½ oz/1 cup) frozen peas

Preheat the oven to 220°C (425°F/Gas 7). Scatter the onion over the bottom of a large roasting tin, lightly spray with oil and place the bay leaves and veal pieces on top. Season with salt and pepper. Roast for 10–15 minutes, or until the veal is browned. Take care that the onion doesn't burn.

Pour the wine over the veal and return to the oven for a further 5 minutes. Reduce the heat to 180°C (350°F/Gas 4), remove the tin from the oven and pour on the tomato, stock and 1 teaspoon of the rosemary. Cover with foil and return to the oven. Cook for 2 hours, or until the veal is starting to fall from the bone. Remove the foil and cook for a further 15 minutes, or until the meat loosens more from the bone and the liquid has evaporated slightly.

Cook the pasta in a large saucepan of rapidly boiling salted water until al dente. Drain well and return to the pan to keep warm. Meanwhile, remove the veal from the oven and cool slightly. Add the peas and remaining rosemary and place over a hotplate. Cook over medium heat for 5 minutes, or until the peas are cooked. Serve the pasta topped with the ragù.

Note: You can either remove the meat from the bone before serving or leave it on.

SERVES 4

Right: Place the bay leaves and veal on top of the onion in the tin and roast until the veal is brown.

Far right: Add the frozen peas to the ragù and cook over medium heat for 5 minutes.

Pasta con Sugo di Pomodoro e Pancetta
Pasta with Creamy Tomato and Bacon Sauce

Streaky bacon is the tail fatty ends of bacon rashers and adds considerable flavour to this dish. However, you can use ordinary bacon slices if you prefer.

400 g (14 oz) pasta
1 tablespoon olive oil
180 g (6¼ oz) streaky bacon, thinly sliced
500 g (1 lb 2 oz) roma (plum) tomatoes, roughly chopped

125 ml (4 fl oz/½ cup) thickened (whipping) cream
2 tablespoons sun-dried tomato pesto
2 tablespoons finely chopped flat-leaf (Italian) parsley
50 g (1¾ oz/½ cup) finely grated parmesan cheese

Cook the pasta in a large saucepan of rapidly boiling salted water until al dente. Drain well and return to the pan to keep warm. Meanwhile, heat the oil in a frying pan, add the bacon and cook over high heat for 2 minutes, or until starting to brown. Reduce the heat to medium, add the tomato and cook, stirring frequently, for 2 minutes, or until the tomato has softened but still holds its shape.

Add the cream and tomato pesto and stir until heated through. Remove from the heat, add the parsley, then toss the sauce through the pasta with the grated parmesan cheese.

SERVES 4

Add the cream and tomato pesto and stir until heated through.

Pasta Cremosa con Piselli e Prosciutto
Creamy Pasta with Peas and Prosciutto

It is important not to overheat or cook the sauce for too long when coating the pasta or the egg will begin to scramble.

100 g (3½ oz) prosciutto, thinly sliced
3 teaspoons oil
2 eggs
250 ml (9 fl oz/1 cup) pouring (whipping) cream
35 g (1¼ oz/⅓ cup) finely grated parmesan cheese

2 tablespoons chopped flat-leaf (Italian) parsley
1 tablespoon snipped chives
250 g (9 oz) fresh or frozen peas
500 g (1 lb 2 oz) pasta shells or gnocchi

Cut the prosciutto into thin strips. Heat the oil in a frying pan over medium heat, add the prosciutto and cook for 2 minutes, or until crisp. Drain on paper towels. Whisk together the eggs, cream, parmesan and herbs in a large bowl.

Bring a large saucepan of salted water to the boil. Add the peas and cook for 5 minutes, or until just tender. Leaving the pan on the heat, use a slotted spoon and transfer the peas to the bowl of cream mixture, and then add 3 tablespoons of the cooking liquid to the same bowl. Using a potato masher or the back of a fork, roughly mash the peas.

Add the pasta to the boiling water and cook until al dente. Drain well, then return to the pan. Add the cream mixture, then warm through over low heat, gently stirring for about 30 seconds until the pasta is coated in the sauce. Season to taste with salt and freshly ground black pepper. Divide among warmed plates, top with the prosciutto and serve immediately.

SERVES 4

Far left: Add the cooked peas to the bowl of eggs, cream, parmesan and herbs and then roughly mash.

Left: Cook the pasta until al dente, then add the cream sauce to the pan of drained pasta.

Food Journey

FRESH PASTA

The only thing more rewarding than making your own pasta is eating it. There's a vast array of good-quality fresh pasta distributed directly from artisan pasta makers and often available at speciality delicatessens.

Once cooked, fresh pasta has a softer texture than dried pasta. This allows it to better absorb the flavours of the sauce it's served with. Fresh pasta can be the perfect foil for both rich creamy sauces and delicate seafood sauces. Ready-made fresh pasta is more expensive than dried, but, made by artisan producers, it is far superior to the entry-level supermarket brands. Buy the best you can afford.

Fresh pasta is generally made with flour, eggs and sometimes a little olive oil or water. The dough can also be flavoured with spinach, tomato, squid ink, saffron or herbs.

The best flour to use is 100 percent durum wheat flour that is very finely milled and classified '00'. Organic eggs really make a difference too.

It is also possible to replace some of the flour with wholemeal (whole grain) or buckwheat flour. Eggless pasta (noodles) can be made using regular flour and is suitable for rich sauces such as ragit.

Fresh filled pasta has a long history, with every region in Italy having its own varieties with unique fillings and shapes. Cappelletti are formed by filling a round of pasta and intricately folding it to form little hats, while tortellini are shaped into 'courtesans' navels'—both types are originally from Emilia. Ravioli are from Liguria; the name comes from the verb 'to wrap'.

Freshly rolled pasta can be dried and stored for up to one week. Many rolled and cut fresh pastas can be stored in the refrigerator, and filled pastas are often sold frozen.

Sheets and cut fresh pasta Cut pastas of various widths have different uses—sheets are used to make lasagne or rotolo (filled pasta rolls) or even modern open ravioli dishes. Long, thin pasta can suit tomato, seafood (such as crab) or light vegetable sauces. Thick cuts of pasta can support chunks of meat or even pieces of seafood. Remember that the simplest sauce will allow the pasta to be the hero of the dish. Types include angel hair, spaghettini, linguine, spaghetti, tagliatelle, fettuccine and pappardelle.

Filled fresh pasta You can buy it ready-made or make your own—there are many possibilities for fillings incorporating cheese, vegetables, meat and seafood. With filled pasta, it can be worth remembering that the pasta can be flavoured too, adding another dimension to the dish before you even add a sauce. Types include square ravioli, round ravioli, agnolotti, tortellini and cappelletti.

Gnocchi Really good gnocchi is made primarily with potato bound with a small amount of flour. It's generally served with a simple sauce, so that when eating you appreciate the light texture of the gnocchi.

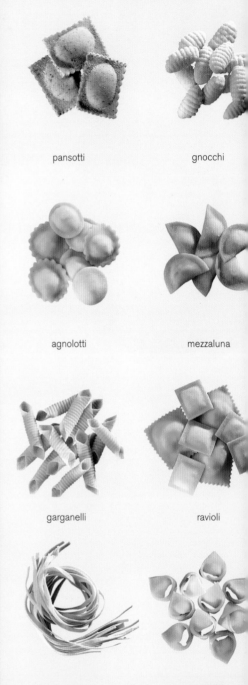

pansotti

gnocchi

agnolotti

mezzaluna

garganelli

ravioli

linguine

cappelletti

tortellini

lasagne

fettucine

tagliatelle

tonarelli

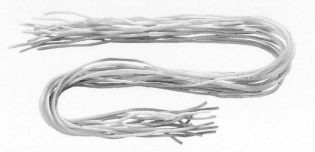

spaghetti

pappardelle

quadrucci

maltagliati

ZITI CON SALSICCIA

Ziti with Sausage

Ziti is a wide tubular pasta which is perfect for meat and vegetable pasta dishes. It gets its name from the word 'zita', meaning bride. In Naples, ziti is the classic pasta served for weddings as the 'zita's pasta'. You could use fettuccine or spaghetti.

1 red capsicum (pepper)
1 green capsicum (pepper)
1 small eggplant (aubergine), sliced
3 tablespoons olive oil
1 onion, sliced
1 garlic clove, crushed
250 g (9 oz) chipolata sausages, sliced
425 g (15 oz) tinned chopped tomatoes

125 ml (4 fl oz/½ cup) red wine
3 tablespoons pitted black olives, halved
1 tablespoon chopped basil
1 tablespoon chopped parsley
500 g (1 lb 2 oz) ziti
2 tablespoons grated parmesan cheese,
  for serving

Cut both capsicums into large flat pieces, removing the seeds and membranes. Place skin side up under a hot grill (broiler) until the skin blackens and blisters. Cool in a plastic bag then peel off the skin. Chop and set aside.

Brush the eggplant with a little oil. Grill (broil) until golden on each side, brushing with more oil as required. Set aside.

Heat the remaining oil in a frying pan. Add the onion and garlic and stir over low heat until the onion is tender. Add the chipolatas and cook until well browned.

Stir in the tomato, wine, olives, basil, parsley and season with salt and pepper. Bring to the boil. Reduce the heat and simmer for 15 minutes. Add the vegetables and heat through. Meanwhile, cook the ziti in a large saucepan of rapidly boiling salted water until al dente. Drain well and return to the pan to keep warm. Toss the vegetables and sauce through the pasta. Sprinkle with parmesan cheese before serving, if desired.

SERVES 4

Far left: Grill the capsicum to remove the skins and then chop the flesh.

Left: Cook the onion until it is tender and then add the sliced chipolatas.

SPAGHETTI CON POLPETTE DI POLLO
Spaghetti with Chicken Meatballs

Wait for the water to come to a rapid boil before adding the spaghetti. If you add the pasta before the water is hot enough it is likely to become sticky and unworkable.

500 g (1 lb 2 oz) minced (ground) chicken
60 g (2¼ oz) grated parmesan cheese, extra, to serve
160 g (5⅔ oz/2 cups) fresh white breadcrumbs
2 garlic cloves, crushed
1 egg
1 tablespoon chopped flat-leaf (Italian) parsley
1 tablespoon chopped sage
3 tablespoons vegetable oil
1 very large handful basil leaves

1 teaspoon coarse ground black pepper
500 g (1 lb 2 oz) spaghetti
2 tablespoons chopped oregano, to serve

TOMATO SAUCE
1 tablespoon olive oil
1 onion, finely chopped
2 kg (4 lb 8 oz) ripe tomatoes, roughly chopped
2 bay leaves

In a large bowl, mix together the mince, parmesan, breadcrumbs, garlic, egg, pepper and herbs. Shape tablespoons of the mixture into small balls and refrigerate for 30 minutes to firm. Heat the oil in a shallow frying pan and fry the balls in batches until golden brown; turn often by shaking the pan. Remove and drain on paper towels.

To make the tomato sauce, heat the oil in a large saucepan, add the onion and fry for 1–2 minutes. Add the tomato and bay leaves, cover and bring to the boil, stirring occasionally. Reduce the heat to low, partially cover and cook for 50–60 minutes.

Add the meatballs, basil leaves and pepper and simmer for 10–15 minutes, uncovered. Meanwhile, cook the spaghetti in a large saucepan of rapidly boiling salted water until al dente. Drain well and return to the pan. Add some sauce to the pasta and toss. Serve the pasta in individual bowls with sauce and meatballs, sprinkled with fresh oregano and a little extra parmesan cheese, if desired.

SERVES 4–6

Right: Shape tablespoons of the mixture into small balls and refrigerate for 30 minutes to firm up.

Far right: Add the meatballs, basil and pepper to the tomato mixture and simmer, uncovered, for 10 minutes.

Penne con Pollo, Asparagi e Formaggio di Capra

Penne with Chicken, Asparagus and Goat's Cheese

You can use feta instead of goat's cheese in this recipe. Using feta will produce a slightly saltier taste than the softer and sweeter flavour of the goat's cheese.

500 g (1 lb 2 oz) penne
350 g (12 oz) asparagus spears
1 tablespoon olive oil
2 boneless, skinless chicken breasts, cut into small cubes
1 tablespoon finely chopped thyme

250 ml (9 fl oz/1 cup) chicken stock
4 tablespoons balsamic vinegar
150 g (5½ oz/1¼ cups) goat's cheese, crumbled

Cook the pasta in a large saucepan of rapidly boiling salted water until al dente. Drain well and return to the pan to keep warm.

Remove the woody ends from the asparagus, cut into short lengths and cook in a saucepan of boiling water for 3 minutes, or until just tender.

Heat the oil in a saucepan over high heat. Add the chicken and cook in batches, stirring occasionally,

for 5 minutes, or until browned. Return all the chicken to the pan. Add the thyme and cook for 1 minute. Add the stock and vinegar and bring to the boil. Reduce the heat and simmer, stirring, for 3–4 minutes, or until the sauce has reduced slightly, then add the asparagus. Toss the pasta with the chicken in a serving bowl and sprinkle with the cheese. Season and serve.

SERVES 4

Far left: The woody ends of the asparagus will snap off easily when you gently bend the stalk.

Left: Simmer the sauce for a few minutes to reduce it slightly before adding the asparagus.

Pasta con Carciofi e Pollo alla Griglia
Pasta with Artichokes and Chargrilled Chicken

Choose an artichoke that feels heavy for its size and has firm, tightly packed leaves that are green (with some purple undertones). Avoid artichokes with leaves that are spongy, loose, dry, splayed, split, pitted or brown at the tips.

1 tablespoon olive oil
3 boneless, skinless chicken breasts
500 g (1 lb 2 oz) pasta
8 prosciutto slices
280 g (10 oz) jar artichokes in oil, drained and quartered, oil reserved

150 g (5½ oz) semi-dried (sun-blushed) tomatoes, thinly sliced
90 g (3¼ oz) baby rocket (arugula) leaves
2–3 tablespoons balsamic vinegar

Lightly brush a chargrill or frying pan with the oil and heat over high heat. Cook the chicken for 5–6 minutes on each side, or until cooked through. Thinly slice and set aside.

Cook the pasta in a large saucepan of rapidly boiling salted water until al dente. Drain well and return to the pan to keep warm.

Meanwhile, place the prosciutto on a grill tray and cook under a hot grill (broiler) for 2 minutes on each side, or until crisp. Cool slightly and break into pieces. Combine the pasta with the chicken, prosciutto, artichokes, tomato and rocket in a bowl and toss. Whisk together 3 tablespoons of the reserved artichoke oil and the balsamic vinegar and toss through the pasta mixture. Season and serve.

SERVES 6

Fry or chargrill the chicken breasts, then thinly slice.

TAGLIATELLE CON FEGATO DI POLLO E CREMA
Tagliatelle with Chicken Livers and Cream

The porous and rough surface of tagliatelle makes it the perfect accompaniment to all sauces. Tagliatelle is available fresh or dried, plain or green (flavoured with spinach) and available in long, thin ribbons of pasta or in curled nests.

2 tablespoons olive oil
1 onion, finely chopped
1 garlic clove, crushed
300 g (10½ oz) chicken livers, chopped into small pieces
250 ml (9 fl oz/1 cup) pouring (whipping) cream
1 tablespoon snipped chives

1 teaspoon wholegrain mustard
2 eggs, beaten
375 g (13 oz) tagliatelle
2 tablespoons grated parmesan cheese,
  for serving

Heat the oil in a large frying pan. Add the onion and garlic and stir over low heat until the onion is tender. Add the chicken livers to the pan and cook gently for 2–3 minutes. Remove from the heat.

Stir in the cream, chives and mustard and season with salt and pepper. Return to the heat and bring the sauce to the boil. Add the eggs, stirring gently. Remove from the heat.

Meanwhile, cook the pasta in a large saucepan of rapidly boiling salted water until al dente. Drain well and return to the pan to keep warm. Add the sauce and toss well to combine. Serve in warmed pasta bowls with grated parmesan, if desired.

SERVES 4

Right: Trim any fat or gristle from the chicken livers before cutting them into small pieces.

Far right: Cook the onion and garlic until the onion is tender and then add the livers.

Chapter 3

PASTA WITH SEAFOOD

When you look at the geography of Italy—surrounded on three sides by ocean—it is easy to see how pasta and seafood have become natural partners. The pairing of fresh crab, clams, prawns or succulent fish with pasta of all shapes and sizes has resulted in some truly spectacular dishes.

Pasta Capelli d'Angelo con Aglio e Capesante
Angel Hair Pasta with Garlic, Scallops and Rocket

For an additional kick, stir in half a teaspoon of dried chilli flakes just before adding the wine and lemon juice to the frying pan.

20 large scallops with roe
250 g (9 oz) angel hair pasta
150 ml (5 fl oz) extra virgin olive oil
2 garlic cloves, finely chopped

3 tablespoons dry white wine
1 tablespoon lemon juice
100 g (3½ oz) baby rocket (arugula) leaves
2 large handfuls chopped coriander (cilantro) leaves

Pull or trim any veins, membrane or hard white muscle from the scallops. Pat the scallops dry with paper towels. Cook the pasta in a large saucepan of rapidly boiling salted water until al dente. Drain well and transfer to a bowl. Toss with 1 tablespoon of the oil.

Meanwhile, heat 1 tablespoon of the oil in a frying pan, add the garlic and cook for a few seconds, or until fragrant. Do not brown. Add the wine and lemon juice, and remove from the heat.

Heat a chargrill pan or barbecue grill plate over high heat and brush with a little oil. Season the scallops with salt and pepper and cook for 1 minute on each side, or until just cooked. Gently reheat the garlic mixture, add the rocket and stir over medium heat for 1–2 minutes, or until wilted. Toss through the pasta and mix together well. Add the remaining oil and half the coriander and mix well. Divide the pasta among four bowls, arrange the scallops over the top and garnish with the remaining coriander.

SERVES 4

Cook the scallops on a chargrill pan or barbecue plate.

Pasta con Salmone Affumicato
Smoked Salmon Pasta

The ridges on the outside of conchiglie pasta shells are perfect for retaining the creamy smoked salmon sauce but you could use lumaconi or cannelloni pasta instead.

500 g (1 lb 2 oz) pasta
1 tablespoon olive oil
4 spring onions (scallions), finely chopped
180 g (6¼ oz/2 cups) button mushrooms, sliced
250 ml (9 fl oz/1 cup) dry white wine
300 ml (10½ fl oz) pouring (whipping) cream

1 tablespoon finely chopped dill
1 tablespoon lemon juice
90 g (3¼ oz) parmesan cheese, grated
200 g (7 oz) smoked salmon, cut into strips
shaved parmesan and lemon wedges, to serve

Cook the pasta in a large saucepan of rapidly boiling salted water until al dente. Drain well and return to the pan to keep warm.

Meanwhile, heat the oil in a small saucepan, add the spring onion and mushrooms and cook over medium heat for 1–2 minutes, or until soft. Add the wine and cream and bring to the boil, then reduce the heat and simmer for 1 minute.

Pour the mushroom sauce over the pasta and stir through the dill and lemon juice. Add the parmesan and stir. Remove from the heat and stir in the smoked salmon. Season with pepper and serve with parmesan shavings and lemon wedges.

SERVES 4

Far left: Cook the spring onion and mushrooms over medium heat until soft.

Left: Add the wine and cream to the saucepan and bring to the boil.

Pappardelle al Tonno e Chermoula
Tuna and Chermoula on Pappardelle

Pappardelle originates from Tuscany, where it is found in many traditional recipes. The glossy, wide ribbons of pasta work perfectly with rich sauces.

500 g (1 lb 2 oz) sweet potato, cut into small cubes
100 ml (3½ fl oz) olive oil
2 large handfuls coriander (cilantro) leaves, finely chopped
2 very large handfuls flat-leaf (Italian) parsley, chopped
3 garlic cloves, crushed

3 teaspoons ground cumin
¾ teaspoon cracked black pepper
3 tablespoons lemon juice
4 x 180 g (6¼ oz) tuna steaks
400 g (14 oz) pappardelle

Preheat the oven to 200°C (400°F/Gas 6). Toss the sweet potato in 2 tablespoons of the oil, place on a baking tray and roast for 25–30 minutes, or until tender.

To make the chermoula, place the coriander, parsley, garlic, cumin and cracked black pepper in a small food processor and process to a rough paste. Transfer to a bowl and stir in the lemon juice and 1 tablespoon of the oil. Place the tuna in a non-metallic bowl, cover with 2 tablespoons of the chermoula and toss until it is evenly coated.

Marinate in the refrigerator for 20 minutes. Meanwhile, cook the pasta in a large saucepan of rapidly boiling salted water until al dente. Drain well and return to the pan to keep warm. Toss with the remaining chermoula and oil.

Heat a lightly oiled chargrill pan over high heat. Cook the tuna for 2 minutes on each side, or until cooked to your liking. Cut into small cubes, toss through the pasta with the sweet potato and serve.

SERVES 4

Far left: Toss the sweet potato in 2 tablespoons of oil and roast until tender.

Left: Cook the tuna for a couple of minutes on each side on a lightly oiled chargrill pan.

Spaghetti ai Frutti di Mare e Sugo al Vino Bianco
Spaghetti with Shellfish and White Wine Sauce

Clams should always be alive when you buy them. Shells should either be tightly closed or, if slightly open, they should close when you tap them firmly. If the shell remains open, the clam should be discarded. Always eat as soon as possible.

500 g (1 lb 2 oz) mussels
1 kg (2 lb 4 oz) clams (vongole)
400 g (14 oz) spaghetti
2 tablespoons olive oil

4 French shallots (eschalots), finely chopped
2 garlic cloves, crushed
250 ml (9 fl oz/1 cup) dry white wine
3 tablespoons chopped flat-leaf (Italian) parsley

Scrub the mussels with a stiff brush and remove any barnacles with a knife. Pull away the hairy beards. Discard any mussels or clams that are broken or open ones that do not close when tapped on the work surface. Wash them all thoroughly under cold running water. Cook the pasta in a large saucepan of rapidly boiling salted water until al dente. Drain well and return to the pan to keep warm.

Meanwhile, heat the oil in a large saucepan over medium heat and cook the shallots for 4 minutes, or until softened. Add the garlic and cook for a further 1 minute. Pour in the wine,

bring to the boil and cook for 2 minutes, or until reduced slightly. Add the clams and mussels, tossing to coat them in the liquid, then cover the pan. Cook, shaking the pan regularly, for about 3 minutes, or until the shells have opened. Discard any clams or mussels that do not open in the cooking time. Toss the clam mixture through the spaghetti, scatter with parsley and transfer to a warmed serving dish. Season and serve with salad and bread.

SERVES 4

Far left: Scrub the mussels and then pull away the hairy beards that grow between the shells.

Left: Cook the mussels and clams in the sauce for 3 minutes, discarding any that don't open.

FRITTATA CON GRANCHI, CAMEMBERT E FUSILLI

Crab, Camembert and Fusilli Frittata

Fusilli is made of strands of pasta twisted into little spring-like shapes and the twists and turns of the pasta are perfect for holding the onion, tomatoes and crabmeat together in this frittata.

90 g (3¼ oz/1 cup) fusilli
1 tablespoon olive oil
1 very small red onion, finely chopped
1 large roma (plum) tomato, roughly chopped
60 g (2¼ oz) semi-dried (sun-blushed) tomatoes, roughly chopped

2 tablespoons finely chopped coriander (cilantro) leaves
150 g (5½ oz/⅔ cup) cooked fresh or tinned crabmeat
150 g (5½ oz) camembert cheese, rind removed, cut into small pieces
6 eggs, plus 2 egg yolks

Cook the pasta in a large saucepan of rapidly boiling salted water until al dente. Drain well and set aside to cool a little.

Meanwhile, heat half the oil in a small frying pan over low heat, add the onion and cook for 4–5 minutes, or until softened but not browned. Transfer to a bowl and add the roma tomato, semi-dried tomato and coriander. Squeeze out any excess moisture from the crabmeat and add to the bowl. Add half the cheese and the cooled pasta.

Mix well. Beat together the 6 eggs and the 2 extra yolks, then stir into the frittata mixture. Season with salt and pepper.

Heat the remaining oil in the frying pan, pour in the frittata mixture and cook over low heat for 25 minutes. Preheat the grill (broiler) to low. Scatter the remaining camembert over the frittata before placing it under the grill for 10–15 minutes, or until cooked and golden brown on top. Remove from the grill and leave for 5 minutes. Cut into slices to serve.

SERVES 4–6

Far left: Add the cooked pasta to the mixture and then the eggs.

Left: Cook the frittata over low heat for 25 minutes and then place under the grill to brown.

Spaghetti con Tonno, Basilico e Capperi

Spaghetti with Tuna, Basil and Capers

A classic Mediterranean combination of flavours. The capers add an important element to the dish—the salted small capers are the best ones to use, rather than those preserved in brine.

500 g (1 lb 2 oz) spaghetti
1 tablespoon extra virgin olive oil
2 garlic cloves, crushed
250 g (9 oz) tinned tuna in brine, drained and broken into chunks

2 very large handfuls basil leaves, torn
4 vine-ripened tomatoes, roughly chopped
2 tablespoons capers, drained and rinsed, roughly chopped
90 g (3¼ oz) parmesan cheese, grated

Cook the pasta in a large saucepan of rapidly boiling salted water until al dente. Drain well and return to the pan to keep warm.

Meanwhile, heat the oil in a small saucepan, add the garlic and tuna and cook over medium heat for a minute, or until the garlic is fragrant and the tuna is warmed through.

Add the tuna mixture, basil, tomato, capers and parmesan to the spaghetti and mix together well. Season and serve with crusty bread.

SERVES 4

Mix together the spaghetti, tuna, basil, tomato, capers and parmesan.

Lasagne ai Frutti di Mare

Seafood Lasagne

To save time blanch the spinach in the same water you cooked the pasta in.

1 tablespoon olive oil
2 garlic cloves, crushed
¼ teaspoon saffron threads
600 g (1 lb 5 oz) bottled tomato pasta sauce
750 g (1 lb 10 oz) mixed raw seafood, cut into bite-sized
   pieces (use scallops and peeled prawns or prepared
   marinara mix)

4 fresh lasagne sheets, cut into twelve 10 x 16 cm
   (4 x 6¼ inch) rectangles
120 g (4¼ oz) English spinach
185 g (6½ oz) mascarpone cheese
90 g (3¼ oz) grated parmesan cheese

Heat the oil in a large saucepan, add the garlic, saffron and pasta sauce, reduce the heat and simmer for 8 minutes, or until thickened slightly. Add the seafood and cook for 2 minutes, or until cooked, then season. Remove from the heat.

Cook the pasta in a large saucepan of boiling salted water for 1–2 minutes, or until al dente. Remove and arrange the sheets on a tray to prevent them sticking. Blanch the spinach in the same saucepan of boiling water for 30 seconds. Remove with tongs, transfer to a colander and drain well.

To assemble, lay a pasta rectangle on each of four ovenproof serving plates. Spread half the mascarpone over the pasta sheets. Top with half the spinach and half the seafood sauce. Sprinkle with one-third of the parmesan. Repeat to give two layers, finishing with a third pasta sheet. Sprinkle with the remaining cheese. Place under a medium grill (broiler) for 2 minutes, or until the cheese is slightly melted. Serve immediately.

SERVES 4

Lay a pasta rectangle on a plate, spread with mascarpone, then spinach and the sauce.

Pasta Capelli d'Angelo Cremosa con Gamberie Aglio

Angel Hair Pasta with Creamy Garlic Prawns

Especially popular throughout the Naples region of Italy, angel hair pasta is like spaghetti, only the sticks are very thin. You can use capellini (slightly thicker), vermicelli (thicker still) or spaghetti as a substitute.

2 tablespoons olive oil
16 raw prawns (shrimp), peeled and deveined
1 leek, chopped
6 garlic cloves, crushed
½ teaspoon dried chilli flakes

125 ml (4 fl oz/½ cup) dry white wine
200 ml (7 fl oz) pouring (whipping) cream
250 g (9 oz) angel hair pasta
3 tablespoons chopped flat-leaf (Italian) parsley

Heat 1 tablespoon of the oil in a frying pan, season the prawns with salt and pepper, add to the pan and cook over high heat for 2–3 minutes, or until cooked through. Remove from the pan, cover and keep warm.

Heat the remaining oil in the same pan, add the leek and cook, stirring, over medium heat for 2–3 minutes, or until softened. Add the garlic and chilli flakes and stir for 1 minute. Pour in the wine, reduce the heat and simmer for 4 minutes, or until reduced. Add the cream and simmer for 3 minutes, or until just thickened.

Meanwhile, cook the pasta in a large saucepan of rapidly boiling salted water until al dente. Drain well and return to the pan to keep warm. Stir the parsley into the sauce and season well. Add the sauce to the pasta and stir to coat. Divide the pasta among bowls and top with the prawns.

SERVES 4

Season the prawns with salt and pepper, then cook over high heat.

Pasta con Acciughe, Broccoli e Basilico
Pasta with Anchovies, Broccoli and Basil

This classic dish is quick and simple yet has a bold flavour. Broccolini can be used instead of the broccoli and you can add more or less chilli to taste. For a variation, substitute chopped pancetta for the anchovies and use a different type of pasta.

600 g (1 lb 5 oz) broccoli, cut into florets
500 g (1 lb 2 oz) orecchiette
1 tablespoon olive oil
4 garlic cloves, finely chopped
8 anchovy fillets, roughly chopped

250 ml (9 fl oz/1 cup) pouring (whipping) cream
2 large handfuls basil, torn
2 teaspoons finely grated lemon zest
100 g (3½ oz/1 cup) parmesan cheese, grated

Blanch the broccoli in a large saucepan of boiling salted water for 3–4 minutes. Remove and plunge into chilled water. Drain well with a slotted spoon. Cook the pasta in a large saucepan of rapidly boiling salted water until al dente. Drain well and return to the pan to keep warm, reserving 2 tablespoons of the cooking water.

Meanwhile, heat the oil in a frying pan over medium heat. Add the garlic and anchovy and cook for 1–2 minutes, or until the garlic begins to turn golden. Add the broccoli and cook for a further 5 minutes. Add the cream and half the basil and cook for 10 minutes, or until the cream has reduced and slightly thickened and the broccoli is very tender.

Purée half the mixture in a food processor until nearly smooth, then return to the pan with the lemon zest, half the parmesan and the reserved cooking water. Stir together well, then season. Add the warm pasta and remaining basil, and toss until well combined. Sprinkle with the remaining parmesan and serve immediately.

SERVES 4–6

Far left: Blanch the broccoli in boiling salted water, then plunge into chilled water and drain well.

Left: Add the cream and half the basil and cook until the sauce has reduced.

Tagliatelle al Salmone e Aneto Cremoso
Tagliatelle with Salmon and Creamy Dill Dressing

Simple yet elegant, this would be an ideal Sunday lunch. You can skin and bone the salmon fillets yourself with a sharp knife and a pair of tweezers or ask your fishmonger to prepare the salmon for you.

350 g (12 oz) fresh tagliatelle
3 tablespoons olive oil
3 x 200 g (7 oz) salmon fillets, skinned and boned
   (ask your fishmonger to do this)
3 garlic cloves, crushed

375 ml (13 fl oz/1 ½ cups) pouring (whipping) cream
1 ½ tablespoons chopped dill
1 teaspoon mustard powder
1 tablespoon lemon juice
30 g (1 oz) parmesan cheese, shaved

Cook the pasta in a large saucepan of rapidly boiling salted water until al dente. Drain well, toss with 1 tablespoon of the oil and return to the pan to keep warm. Meanwhile, heat the remaining oil in a large deep frying pan and cook the salmon for 2 minutes on each side, or until crisp on the outside but still pink on the inside. Remove from the pan, cut into small cubes and keep warm.

In the same pan, cook the garlic for 30 seconds, or until fragrant. Add the cream, dill and mustard powder, bring to the boil, then reduce the heat and simmer, stirring, for 4–5 minutes, or until thickened. Season.

Add the salmon and any juices plus the lemon juice to the creamy dill sauce and stir until warmed through. Gently toss the sauce and salmon through the pasta and divide among four serving bowls. Sprinkle with the parmesan (if desired) and serve.

SERVES 4

Right: Cook the salmon for 2 minutes on each side to sear it, then cut into cubes.

Far right: Add the salmon and any juices to the sauce, with the lemon juice.

Chapter 4

Vegetarian Pasta

〰️

*While the Italian cook makes good use of pantry staples such as canned
tomatoes and olive oil, it is the fresh vegetables and herbs that lift the
dishes into the sublime. Tomatoes, peppers and artichokes ripen
under the Mediterranean sun and, tossed together with a bowl of pasta,
are as colourful and delicious as they are good for you.*

Fettuccine con Zucchine
Fettuccine with Zucchini

You can use either tagliatelle or the slightly narrower fettuccine ribbons in this recipe. Pappardelle, which is slightly wider than tagliatelle, also works well in this dish.

500 g (1 lb 2 oz) tagliatelle or fettuccine
60 g (2¼ oz/¼ cup) salted butter
2 garlic cloves, crushed
500 g (1 lb 2 oz) zucchini (courgettes), grated

75 g (2½ oz/¾ cup) grated parmesan cheese
250 ml (9 fl oz/1 cup) olive oil
16 basil leaves

Cook the pasta in a large saucepan of rapidly boiling salted water until al dente. Drain well and return to the pan to keep warm.

Meanwhile, heat the butter in a deep heavy-based saucepan over low heat until it is foaming. Add the garlic and cook for 1 minute. Add the zucchini and cook, stirring occasionally, for 1–2 minutes or until the zucchini has softened.

Add the sauce to the pasta. Add the parmesan cheese and toss well.

To make the basil leaves crisp, heat the oil in a small frying pan, add two leaves at a time and cook for 1 minute or until crisp. Drain on paper towels. Serve with the pasta.

SERVES 4–6

Far left: Coarsely grate the zucchini and then fry with the garlic until softened.

Left: Fry the basil leaves in a little oil until they are crisp; then drain on paper towels.

Gnocchi di Patate con Sugo di Pomodoro e Basilico
Potato Gnocchi with Tomato and Basil Sauce

To achieve the best results, it is important to choose a potato with minimum water content. Gnocchi freeze really well uncooked so you can make double the quantity and freeze for later use.

TOMATO SAUCE
1 tablespoon oil
1 onion, chopped
1 celery stalk, chopped
2 carrots, chopped
850 g (1 lb 14 oz) tinned chopped tomatoes
1 teaspoon sugar
1 very large handful basil, chopped

1 kg (2 lb 4 oz) all-purpose potatoes, roughly chopped
30 g (1 oz) salted butter
250 g (9 oz/2 cups) plain (all-purpose) flour
2 eggs, beaten
grated parmesan cheese, for serving

To make the tomato sauce, heat the oil in a large frying pan and cook the onion, celery and carrots for 5 minutes, stirring regularly. Add the tomato and sugar and season. Bring to the boil, reduce the heat to very low and simmer for 20 minutes. Mix until smooth in a food processor. Add the basil leaves and set aside.

To make the gnocchi, cook the potatoes in boiling water for 15 minutes or until very tender. Drain well and mash until smooth. Using a wooden spoon, stir in the butter and the flour, then mix in the eggs. Leave to cool.

Turn the potato mixture out onto a floured surface and divide in two. Roll each half into a long sausage shape. Cut into 3–4 cm (1¼–1½ inch) pieces and press each piece with the back of a fork to give the gnocchi ridges.

Bring a large saucepan of salted water to the boil, add the gnocchi and cook for 3 minutes, or until they rise to the surface. Drain with a slotted spoon and serve with the tomato sauce and grated parmesan cheese.

SERVES 4–6

Right: Use a wooden spoon to mix the eggs into the mashed potato.

Far right: Press each piece of gnocchi with the back of a fork to give the traditional ridges.

Tagliatelle con Asparagi, Piselli e Sugo alle Erbe

Tagliatelle with Asparagus, Peas and Herb sauce

It is best to use thin asparagus but you can use larger asparagus if you remove the tough bases first. To do this, gently bend the spear and it will break at the natural division between the woody base and tender upper part of the stem.

375 g (13 oz) tagliatelle
2 leeks, thinly sliced
250 ml (9 fl oz/1 cup) chicken or vegetable stock
3 garlic cloves, crushed
250 g (9 oz/1½ cups) shelled fresh peas
1 tablespoon finely chopped mint
400 g (14 oz) asparagus spears, cut into
   5 cm (2 inch) lengths

15 g (½ oz) finely chopped parsley
30 g (1 oz) shredded basil
4 tablespoons pouring (whipping) cream
pinch of grated nutmeg
1 tablespoon grated parmesan cheese
2 tablespoons extra virgin olive oil, to serve

Cook the pasta in a large saucepan of rapidly boiling salted water until al dente. Drain well and return to the pan to keep warm.

Put the leeks and 125 ml (4 fl oz/½ cup) of the stock in a large, deep, frying pan. Cook over low heat, stirring often, for 4–5 minutes. Stir in the garlic, peas and mint and cook for 1 minute. Add the remaining stock and 125 ml (4 fl oz/½ cup) water and bring to the boil. Simmer for

5 minutes. Add the asparagus, parsley and basil and season well. Simmer for 3–4 minutes, or until the asparagus is just tender. Gradually increase the heat to thicken the sauce until it will just coat a spoon. Stir in the cream, nutmeg and parmesan and season.

Add the sauce to the tagliatelle and toss lightly to coat. Serve drizzled with the extra virgin olive oil.

SERVES 4

Right: Stir the garlic, peas and mint into the stock and leek mixture.

Far right: Stir in the cream, nutmeg and grated parmesan and check the seasoning.

Linguine con Sugo ai Peperoni Rossi
Linguine with Red Capsicum Sauce

If you prefer the dish to have a stronger capsicum flavour, or want a healthier option, you can omit the cream.

3 red capsicums (peppers)
3 tablespoons olive oil
1 large onion, sliced
2 garlic cloves, crushed

¼–½ teaspoon chilli flakes or powder
125 ml (4 fl oz/½ cup) pouring (whipping) cream
2 tablespoons chopped oregano
500 g (1 lb 2 oz) linguine or spaghetti

Halve each capsicum, removing the membrane and seeds and cut into large pieces. Place skin side up under a hot grill (broiler) and cook for 8 minutes or until black and blistered. Cover with a damp tea towel (dish towel) and allow to cool. Peel off the skin and cut the capsicum into thin strips.

Heat the oil in a large heavy-based saucepan. Add the onion and cook, stirring, over low heat for 8 minutes or until soft. Add the capsicum, garlic, chilli flakes or powder and cream and cook for 2 minutes, stirring occasionally. Season and add the oregano.

Meanwhile, cook the pasta in a large saucepan of rapidly boiling salted water until al dente. Drain well and return to the pan to keep warm. Add the sauce to the pasta and toss well before serving.

Note: If you use dried oregano use about one-third of the quantity as dried herbs are stronger in flavour.

SERVES 4–6

Grill the capsicum until the skin is blackened and will peel away easily.

Fettuccine con Patate Dolci, Feta e Olive
Fettuccine with Sweet Potato, Feta and Olives

1.5 kg (3 lb 5 oz) orange sweet potato, cut into
   small cubes
4 tablespoons olive oil
4 garlic cloves, crushed
2 tablespoons salted butter

4 red onions, sliced into thin wedges
500 g (1 lb 2 oz) fresh plain or spinach fettuccine
400 g (14 oz) soft feta cheese, diced
200 g (7 oz) small black olives
2 large handfuls basil, torn

Preheat the oven to 200°C (400°F/Gas 6). Place the sweet potato, oil and garlic in a bowl and toss to coat the sweet potato. Lay out the sweet potato in a roasting tin and roast for 15 minutes. Turn and roast for another 15 minutes, until tender and golden—make sure the sweet potato is not too soft or it will not hold its shape. Keep warm.

Meanwhile, melt the butter in a deep frying pan and cook the onion over low heat, stirring occasionally, for 25–30 minutes, or until soft and slightly caramelised.

Cook the pasta in a large saucepan of rapidly boiling salted water until al dente. Drain well and return to the pan. Add the onion to the pasta and toss together. Add the sweet potato, feta, olives and basil and gently toss. Serve drizzled with extra virgin olive oil.

SERVES 6

Cook the onion in the butter over low heat until soft
and caramelised.

Penne con Sugo di Lenticchie Rustiche

Penne with Rustic Lentil Sauce

Not all pasta sauces need to be laden with tomatoes, and this tasty combination of lentils and vegetables is as comforting as it is delicious. It's an ideal meal when the weather starts to get a little cooler.

1 litre (35 fl oz/4 cups) vegetable or chicken stock
350 g (12 oz) penne
4 tablespoons virgin olive oil, plus extra for serving
1 onion, chopped
2 carrots, diced

3 celery stalks, diced
3 garlic cloves, crushed
1 tablespoon chopped thyme, plus 1 teaspoon, extra
400 g (14 oz) tinned lentils, drained

Boil the chicken stock in a large saucepan for 10 minutes, or until reduced by half. Meanwhile, cook the pasta in a large saucepan of rapidly boiling salted water until al dente. Drain well and toss with 2 tablespoons of the olive oil.

Heat the remaining oil in a large, deep frying pan, add the onion, carrot and celery and cook over medium heat for 10 minutes, or until browned. Add two-thirds of the crushed garlic and

1 tablespoon of the thyme and cook for a further 1 minute. Add the stock, bring to the boil and cook for 8 minutes, or until tender. Stir in the lentils and heat through.

Stir in the remaining garlic and thyme and season well—the stock should be slightly syrupy at this point. Combine the pasta with the lentil sauce in a large bowl and drizzle with virgin olive oil to serve.

SERVES 4

Stir the remaining garlic and thyme into the sauce and season well.

ROTELLE CON CECI, POMODORI E PREZZEMOLO
Rotelle with Chickpeas, Tomato and Parsley

For a change from regular tomatoes, you can try roma (plum) tomatoes. They are firm-fleshed, with few seeds and have a rich flavour when cooked.

375 g (13 oz) rotelle
1 tablespoon ground cumin
125 ml (4 fl oz/½ cup) olive oil
1 red onion, halved and thinly sliced
3 garlic cloves, crushed

400 g (14 oz) tinned chickpeas, drained
3 large tomatoes, diced
1 large handful chopped flat-leaf (Italian) parsley
3 tablespoons lemon juice

Cook the pasta in a large saucepan of rapidly boiling salted water until al dente. Drain well and return to the pan to keep warm.

Meanwhile, heat a large frying pan over medium heat, add the cumin and cook, tossing, for 1 minute, or until fragrant. Remove from the pan. Heat half the oil in the same pan and cook the onion over medium heat for 2–3 minutes, or until soft. Stir in the garlic, chickpeas, tomato and parsley and stir until warmed through. Gently toss through the pasta.

Place the lemon juice, cumin and remaining oil in a jar with a lid and shake together well. Add the dressing to the saucepan with the pasta and chickpea mixture, return to the stovetop over low heat and stir until warmed through. Season well with salt and freshly ground black pepper. Serve hot with grated parmesan, or serve cold. If serving cold, rinse the pasta under cold water before adding the chickpea mixture and do not return to the heat.

SERVES 4

Far left: Add the garlic, chickpeas, tomato and parsley and stir to warm through.

Left: Mix together the lemon juice, cumin and remaining oil to make a dressing.

Patate Dolci Arrostite e Polpette ai Ditalini
Roasted Sweet Potato and Ditalini Patties

Choose firm, smooth, dark sweet potatoes without wrinkles, bruises, sprouts, or decay. Even if you cut out a decayed spot it might have already caused the whole potato to take on an unpleasant flavour.

800 g (1 lb 12 oz) orange sweet potatoes
90 g (3¼ oz/½ cup) ditalini
30 g (1 oz) pine nuts, toasted
2 garlic cloves, crushed
4 tablespoons finely chopped basil

60 g (2¼ oz) grated parmesan cheese
35 g (1¼ oz/⅓ cup) dry breadcrumbs
plain (all-purpose) flour, for dusting
olive oil, for shallow-frying

Preheat the oven to 250°C (500°F/Gas 9). Pierce the whole sweet potatoes several times with a fork, then place in a roasting tin and roast for about 1 hour, or until soft. Remove from the oven and cool. Meanwhile, cook the pasta in a large saucepan of rapidly boiling salted water until al dente. Drain well and rinse under cold water.

Peel the sweet potato and mash with a potato masher or fork. Add the pine nuts, garlic, basil, parmesan, breadcrumbs and the pasta and mix together. Season.

Shape the mixture into eight even patties with floured hands, then lightly dust the patties with

flour. Heat the oil in a large frying pan and cook the patties in batches over medium heat for 2 minutes on each side, or until golden and heated through. Drain on crumpled paper towels, sprinkle with salt and serve immediately.

Note: If you don't have much time, drop spoonfuls of the mixture into the pan and flatten with an oiled spatula.

Variation: The patties are great with aïoli—mix 1 clove of crushed garlic into 90 g (3¼ oz/⅓ cup) mayonnaise with a squeeze of lemon juice and season well.

SERVES 4

Far left: Roast the sweet potatoes in their skins for an hour and then pierce to check they are soft.

Left: Keep your hands lightly floured when shaping the patties so they don't stick.

Pasta alla Campagnola

Farmhouse Pasta

It is a good idea to wear rubber gloves when chopping or seeding the chillies for this recipe. This will help you to avoid skin irritation and rashes.

375 g (13 oz) pasta
1 large all-purpose potato, cut into small cubes
400 g (14 oz) broccoli
4 tablespoons olive oil

3 garlic cloves, crushed
1 small red chilli, finely chopped
800 g (1 lb 12 oz) tinned chopped tomatoes
30 g (1 oz/⅓ cup) grated pecorino cheese

Bring a large saucepan of salted water to the boil and cook the pasta and potato together for 8–10 minutes, or until the pasta is al dente. Drain and return to the saucepan. Meanwhile, trim the broccoli into florets and discard the stems. Place in a saucepan of boiling water and cook for 1–2 minutes, then drain and plunge into iced water. Drain and add to the cooked pasta and potato.

Heat the oil in a saucepan, add the garlic and chilli and cook for 30 seconds. Add the tomato and simmer for 5 minutes, or until slightly reduced and thickened. Season to taste with salt and freshly ground black pepper.

Pour the tomato mixture over the pasta, potato and broccoli. Toss well and stir over low heat until warmed through. Serve sprinkled with grated pecorino cheese.

SERVES 4

Right: Blanch the broccoli in boiling water for a couple of minutes then cool in iced water.

Far right: Simmer the tomato sauce for 5 minutes, or until it has thickened.

SPAGHETTI CON ERBE DA CUCINA, SPINACINI E AGLIO TRITATO
Spaghetti with Herbs, Baby Spinach and Garlic Crumbs

375 g (13 oz) spaghetti
125 g (4½ oz) day-old crusty Italian bread, crusts
  removed
100 ml (3½ fl oz) extra virgin olive oil, plus extra
  for serving
4 garlic cloves, finely chopped

400 g (14 oz) baby English spinach leaves
4 tablespoons chopped basil
2 large handfuls chopped flat-leaf (Italian) parsley
1 tablespoon thyme leaves
30 g (1 oz) shaved parmesan cheese, to serve

Cook the pasta in a large saucepan of rapidly
boiling salted water until al dente. Drain well and
return to the pan to keep warm, reserving 125 ml
(4 fl oz/½ cup) of the cooking water.

To make the garlic breadcrumbs, mix the bread in
a food processor or blender until coarse crumbs
form. Heat 1 tablespoon of oil in a saucepan.
Add the breadcrumbs and half the garlic and toss
for 2–3 minutes, or until lightly golden. Remove
and clean the pan with paper towels.

Heat 2 tablespoons of the oil in the same pan. Add
the spinach and remaining garlic, toss together for
1 minute, then add the herbs. Cook, tossing
frequently, for a further 1 minute to wilt the herbs
a little and to heat through. Toss through the pasta
with the remaining oil and reserved pasta water.
Divide among serving bowls and scatter with the
garlic breadcrumbs. Serve hot sprinkled with
parmesan and drizzled with extra virgin olive oil.

SERVES 4

Far left: Cook the spaghetti until al dente, then drain and return
to the pan to keep warm.

Left: Add the spinach and remaining garlic to the oil in the pan
and toss together over the heat.

Lasagne con Funghi Selvatici
Free-form Wild Mushroom Lasagne

Shiitake mushrooms have a somewhat spongy texture, with a rich 'meaty' flavour. Discard any that are wrinkled or have slimy spots and choose ones that are firm, plump and clean.

10 g (¼ oz) dried porcini mushrooms
350 g (12 oz) wild mushrooms (such as shiitake, oyster, Swiss brown)
30 g (1 oz) salted butter
1 small onion, halved and thinly sliced
1 tablespoon chopped thyme
3 egg yolks
125 ml (4 fl oz/½ cup) thickened (whipping) cream
100 g (3½ oz/1 cup) grated parmesan cheese
8 fresh lasagne sheets (10 x 25 cm/4 x 10 inches)

Soak the porcini in 3 tablespoons boiling water for 15 minutes. Strain through a sieve, reserving the liquid. Cut the larger of all the mushrooms in half. Heat the butter in a frying pan and cook the onion over medium heat for 1–2 minutes, or until just soft. Add the thyme and mushrooms (including the porcini) and cook for 1–2 minutes, or until softened. Pour in the reserved mushroom liquid and cook for 1–2 minutes, or until the liquid has evaporated. Set aside.

Beat the egg yolks, cream and half the parmesan in a large bowl. Cook the lasagne sheets in a large saucepan of boiling water for 2–3 minutes, stirring gently. Drain well and toss the sheets gently through the egg mixture while hot. Reheat the mushrooms quickly. To serve, place a sheet of folded lasagne on a plate, top with some mushrooms, then another sheet of folded lasagne. Drizzle with any remaining egg mixture and sprinkle with the remaining parmesan.

SERVES 4

Far leftt: Add the thyme and all the mushrooms to the pan, then add the porcini soaking liquid.

Left: Toss the lasagne sheets gently though the egg, cream and parmesan mixture.

Chapter 5

FILLED PASTA

◇◇◇◇◇◇◇◇◇◇◇◇◇◇◇◇◇◇◇◇◇◇◇◇◇◇◇◇◇◇

*Make your own pasta dough and shape it into delicate pillows of
ravioli, horseshoe tortellini or cannelloni tubes. Then fill those tiny parcels
of pasta with just about any of your favourite ingredients, from puréed
vegetables, spinach and ricotta, to robust meat sauces.*

AGNOLOTTI AL POLLO

Chicken Agnolotti

Agnolotti are traditionally made by folding small, thinly rolled rounds of pasta dough over fillings into a half-moon shape, and pressing the edges to seal.

PASTA
250 g (9 oz/2 cups) plain (all-purpose) flour
3 eggs
1 tablespoon olive oil
1 egg yolk, extra

FILLING
125 g (4½ oz) minced (ground) chicken
75 g (2½ oz) ricotta or cottage cheese
60 g (2¼ oz) chicken livers, trimmed and chopped
30 g (1 oz) prosciutto, chopped
1 slice salami, chopped
2 tablespoons grated parmesan cheese

1 egg, beaten
1 tablespoon chopped parsley
1 garlic clove, crushed
¼ teaspoon mixed (pumpkin pie) spice

TOMATO SAUCE
2 tablespoons olive oil
1 onion, finely chopped
2 garlic cloves, crushed
850 g (1 lb 14 oz) tinned chopped tomatoes
1 handful chopped basil
½ teaspoon mixed herbs

To make the pasta, sift the flour and a pinch of salt onto a board. Make a well in the centre of the flour. In a bowl, whisk together the eggs, oil and 1 tablespoon water. Add the egg mixture gradually to flour, working in with your hands until mixture forms a ball. Knead on a lightly floured surface for 5 minutes, or until smooth and elastic. Place the dough in a lightly oiled bowl and cover with plastic wrap. Allow to stand for 30 minutes.

To make the filling, process all filling ingredients in processor until finely chopped.

To make the sauce, heat the oil in a saucepan. Add the onion and garlic and stir over low heat until onion is tender. Increase heat, add tomatoes, basil, herbs and season. Stir. Bring to the boil. Reduce heat and simmer for 15 minutes. Remove from the heat.

Roll out half the dough until 1 mm (¹⁄₁₆ inch) thick. Cut into 10 cm (4 inch) strips. Place teaspoons of filling at 5 cm (2 inch) intervals down one side of each strip. Whisk together extra egg yolk and 3 tablespoons water. Brush along one side of dough and between the filling. Fold dough over filling. Press edges together. Cut between the mounds of filling with a knife or a fluted pastry cutter.

Cook ravioli in batches in rapidly boiling salted water for 10 minutes. Reheat the sauce in a large pan. Add the cooked ravioli and toss well until the sauce is evenly distributed. Simmer, stirring, for 5 minutes, then serve.

SERVES 4

TORTELLINI DI VITELLO CON SUGO AI FUNGHI
Veal Tortellini with Creamy Mushroom Sauce

A good-quality dry white wine is the secret to this tasty sauce. Add some to the sauce and drink the rest for dinner. You can use a marsala instead of white wine.

500 g (1 lb 2 oz) veal tortellini
3 tablespoons olive oil
600 g (1 lb 5 oz) Swiss brown mushrooms, thinly sliced
2 garlic cloves, crushed
125 ml (4 fl oz/½ cup) dry white wine

300 ml (10½ fl oz) thickened (whipping) cream
pinch of grated nutmeg
3 tablespoons finely chopped flat-leaf (Italian) parsley
30 g (1 oz) grated parmesan cheese, to serve

Cook the pasta in a large saucepan of rapidly boiling salted water until al dente. Drain well and return to the pan to keep warm. Meanwhile, heat the oil in a frying pan over medium heat. Add the mushrooms and cook, stirring occasionally and gently, for 5 minutes, or until softened. Add the garlic and cook for 1 minute, then stir in the wine and cook for 5 minutes, or until the liquid has reduced by half.

Add the cream, nutmeg and parsley, stir to combine and cook for 3–5 minutes, or until the sauce thickens slightly. Season with salt and freshly ground black pepper. Divide the tortellini among four serving plates and spoon on the mushroom sauce. Sprinkle with parmesan cheese (if desired) and serve.

SERVES 4

Far left: Heat the oil in a frying pan, add the mushrooms and cook until softened.

Left: Add the cream, nutmeg and parsley and stir until the sauce thickens slightly.

Ravioli con Ripieno alle Erbe
Herb-filled Ravioli

300 g (10½ oz) plain (all-purpose) flour
3 eggs, beaten
3 tablespoons olive oil
250 g (9 oz/1 cup) ricotta cheese
2 tablespoons grated parmesan cheese

2 teaspoons snipped chives
1 tablespoon chopped flat-leaf (Italian) parsley
2 teaspoons chopped basil
1 teaspoon chopped lemon thyme or thyme
1 egg, beaten, extra

Sift the flour into a bowl and make a well in the centre. Gradually mix in the eggs and oil. Turn out onto a lightly floured surface and knead for 6 minutes, or until elastic. Cover with plastic wrap and leave for 30 minutes. To make the filling, mix the ricotta, parmesan and herbs. Season well.

Divide the dough into four portions and shape each into a log. Cover portions. Take one portion and flatten with a rolling pin. Roll out each portion as thinly as possible into rectangles, making 2 slightly larger and wider than the others.

Spread one of the smaller sheets out. Spoon 1 teaspoon of the filling at 5 cm (2 inch) intervals. Brush the egg between the filling along the cutting lines. Place a larger sheet on top. Press the two sheets together along the cutting lines. Cut the ravioli with a pastry cutter or knife. Transfer to a lightly floured baking tray. Repeat with the remaining sheets and filling. Cook the ravioli in a large saucepan of rapidly boiling water for 5–8 minutes and top with a sauce of your choice.

SERVES 4

Ravioli alle Erbe
Ravioli with Herbs

As a variation, you can use fresh coriander (cilantro) instead of parsley.

2 tablespoons olive oil
1 garlic clove, halved
800 g (1 lb 12 oz) ravioli
60 g (2¼ oz) salted butter, chopped

2 tablespoons chopped parsley
1 large handful chopped basil
2 tablespoons snipped chives

Combine the oil and garlic in a small bowl and set aside. Cook the pasta in a large saucepan of rapidly boiling salted water until al dente. Drain well and return to the pan to keep warm.

Add the oil to the pasta, discarding the garlic. Add the butter and herbs and toss well before serving.

PICTURE ON OPPOSITE PAGE

SERVES 4-6

Ravioli alla Barbabietola con Burro e Salvia
Beetroot Ravioli with Sage Burnt Butter

340 g (11¾ oz) jar baby beetroots (beets) in
    sweet vinegar
40 g (1½ oz) grated parmesan cheese
250 g (9 oz/1 cup) ricotta cheese
750 g (1 lb 10 oz) fresh lasagne sheets

fine cornmeal, for sprinkling
200 g (7 oz) salted butter, chopped
8 sage leaves, torn
2 garlic cloves, crushed

Drain the beetroot, then grate it into a bowl. Add the parmesan cheese and ricotta and mix well. Lay a sheet of pasta on a flat surface and place evenly spaced tablespoons of the beetroot mixture on the pasta to give 12 mounds—four across and three down. Flatten the mounds slightly. Lightly brush the edges of the pasta sheet and around each pile of filling with water.

Place a second sheet of pasta over the top and gently press around each mound to seal and enclose the filling. Using a fluted pastry cutter or sharp knife, cut the pasta into 12 ravioli. Lay them

out separately on a lined tray that has been sprinkled with the cornmeal. Repeat with the remaining filling and lasagne sheets to make 24 ravioli. Gently remove any excess air bubbles after cutting so that they are completely sealed. Cook the pasta in a large saucepan of rapidly boiling salted water until al dente. Drain well and return to the pan to keep warm. Melt the butter in a saucepan and cook for 3–4 minutes, or until golden brown. Remove from the heat, stir in the sage and garlic and spoon over the ravioli. Sprinkle with shaved parmesan to serve.

SERVES 4

Far left: Brush between the mounds of filling with a little water so the pasta will stick.

Left: Remove the melted butter from the heat and stir in the sage and garlic.

Tortellini con Speck, Asparagi e Pomodoro
Tortellini with Speck, Asparagus and Tomato

Made from the hind pork leg, speck is a fatty bacon that is smoked over beechwood with herbs and spices. It is used primarily to flavour soups and sauces.

200 g (7 oz) piece speck (skin removed if it has one)
4 tomatoes
300 g (10½ oz) asparagus spears, cut into short lengths
500 g (1 lb 2 oz) cheese tortellini
1 tablespoon olive oil

1 red onion, thinly sliced
1 tablespoon tomato paste (concentrated purée)
125 ml (4 fl oz/½ cup) chicken stock
2 teaspoons thyme leaves

Chop the speck in a food processor. Score a cross in the base of each tomato, place in a heatproof bowl and cover with boiling water. Leave for 1 minute, then plunge into cold water and peel the skin away from the cross. Roughly chop the tomatoes.

Cook the asparagus in a large saucepan of boiling water for 2 minutes, or until just tender, then remove and refresh in cold water. Drain. Cook the pasta in a large saucepan of rapidly boiling salted water until al dente. Drain well and return to the pan to keep warm.

Meanwhile, heat the oil in a saucepan, add the speck and onion and cook, stirring, over medium heat for 2–3 minutes, or until the onion is soft. Add the tomato, tomato paste, stock and thyme and season to taste with salt and freshly ground black pepper. Cook, stirring, for 5 minutes. Add the pasta and asparagus to the tomato mixture and stir over low heat until warmed through. Divide among warmed bowls and serve.

SERVES 4–6

Right: Remove skin from speck if it has one. Chop the speck in a food processor using the pulse button.

Far right: Blanch the asparagus in hot and then cold water so it keeps its bright colour.

Tortellini di Pollo al Pomodoro
Chicken Tortellini with Tomato Sauce

There are many types of fresh tortellini readily available at the supermarket so experiment and find one you like if you don't want to make your own.

PASTA
250 g (9 oz/2 cups) plain (all-purpose) flour
3 eggs
1 tablespoon olive oil

FILLING
20 g (¾ oz) salted butter
80 g (2¾ oz) boneless, skinless chicken breast, cubed
2 slices pancetta, chopped
50 g (1¾ oz/½ cup) grated parmesan cheese
½ teaspoon nutmeg
1 egg, lightly beaten

TOMATO SAUCE
4 tablespoons olive oil
1.5 kg (3 lb 5 oz) ripe tomatoes, peeled and chopped
1 large handful chopped oregano
50 g (1¾ oz/½ cup) grated parmesan cheese

100 g (3½ oz) fresh bocconcini (fresh baby mozzarella cheese), thinly sliced, to serve

To make the pasta, sift the flour and a pinch of salt into a bowl. Make a well in the centre. In a bowl, whisk together the eggs, oil and 1 tablespoon water. Add gradually to the flour, mixing to a firm dough. Make a ball, adding a little extra water if necessary. Knead on a lightly floured surface for 5 minutes, or until the dough is elastic. Place in a lightly oiled bowl, cover with plastic wrap. Leave for 30 minutes.

To make the filling, heat the butter in a frying pan, add the chicken and cook until golden brown. Drain. Process the chicken and pancetta in a food processor until finely chopped. Transfer to a bowl and add the cheese, nutmeg and egg. Set aside.

Roll out dough very thinly on a lightly floured surface. Using a floured cutter, cut into 5 cm

(2 inch) rounds. Spoon about ½ teaspoon of filling into the centre of each round. Fold the rounds in half to form semi-circles, pressing the edges together firmly. Wrap each semi-circle around your finger to form a ring and then press the ends of the dough together firmly.

To make the sauce, place the oil, tomato and oregano in a frying pan and cook over high heat for 10 minutes. Stir in the parmesan. Set aside.

Cook the tortellini in two batches in rapidly boiling water for about 6 minutes for each batch. Drain well and return to the pan. Reheat the sauce, add to tortellini and toss to combine. Divide the tortellini among individual bowls, top with the bocconcini and allow the cheese to melt a little before serving.

SERVES 4

Ham Tortellini with Nutty Herb Sauce

500 g (1 lb 2 oz) ham and cheese tortellini
60 g (2¼ oz) salted butter
125 g (4½ oz/1 cup) walnuts, chopped
100 g (3½ oz/⅔ cup) pine nuts

2 tablespoons finely chopped flat-leaf (Italian) parsley
2 teaspoons chopped thyme
60 g (2¼ oz/¼ cup) ricotta cheese
3 tablespoons pouring (whipping) cream

Cook the pasta in a large saucepan of rapidly boiling salted water until al dente. Drain well and return to the pan to keep warm. Meanwhile, heat the butter in a frying pan over medium heat until foaming. Add the walnuts and pine nuts and stir for 5 minutes, or until golden brown. Add the parsley and thyme and season to taste.

Beat the ricotta and cream together. Then add it to the nutty butter, stirring constantly. Add this nutty sauce to the pasta and toss. Divide among serving bowls and top with the ricotta cream.

SERVES 4–6

Heat the butter until foaming and then cook the walnuts and pine nuts until golden.

Ravioli di Spinaci con Pomodori e Formaggio di Capra

Spinach Ravioli with Tomatoes and Goat's Cheese

If you only have unpitted olives available, remove the pit by making a small x-shaped cut with the tip of a sharp knife on one end of the olive; then pinch the other end between your thumb and forefinger until the pit pops out.

4 roma (plum) tomatoes
6 garlic cloves, unpeeled and bruised
4 tablespoons extra virgin olive oil
2½ teaspoons caster (superfine) sugar
500 g (1 lb 2 oz) spinach ravioli

2 tablespoons red wine vinegar
90 g (3¼ oz) pitted kalamata olives
100 g (3½ oz) baby English spinach leaves
100 g (3½ oz) goat's cheese, crumbled

Preheat the oven to 190°C (375°F/Gas 5). Cut each tomato into eight wedges. Place on a large lightly greased baking tray, with the garlic cloves. Drizzle with 1 tablespoon of the olive oil, then sprinkle with 1 teaspoon of the sugar. Season with salt and pepper. Roast for 1 hour, or until softened and caramelised. Remove and keep warm.

Just before the tomatoes are ready, cook the pasta in a large saucepan of rapidly boiling salted water until al dente. Drain well and place in a large bowl. Remove the skins from the garlic.

To make the dressing, combine the remaining extra virgin olive oil with the vinegar, peeled roasted garlic and the remaining sugar in a screw-top jar and shake well. Pour over the pasta and toss gently. Add the olives, spinach, goat's cheese and roasted tomato and toss together. Serve immediately.

SERVES 4

Right: Roast the tomato wedges on a baking tray with the bruised garlic cloves.

Far right: When the garlic is roasted it will be easy to peel the skin away.

Ravioli di Pollo con Sugo di Pomodoro Fresco
Chicken Ravioli with Fresh Tomato Sauce

Make an extra batch of the tomato sauce and freeze it for later as it will pair with any type of pasta or you can spread it over a pizza base. Won ton wrappers are readily available in the refrigerated section of supermarkets.

TOMATO SAUCE
1 tablespoon olive oil
1 large onion, chopped
2 garlic cloves, crushed
90 g (3¼ oz/⅓ cup) tomato paste (concentrated purée)
3 tablespoons dry red wine
170 ml (5½ fl oz/⅔ cup) chicken stock
2 tomatoes, chopped
1 tablespoon chopped basil

RAVIOLI
200 g (7 oz) minced (ground) chicken
1 tablespoon chopped basil
25 g (1 oz/¼ cup) grated parmesan cheese
3 spring onions (scallions), finely chopped
50 g (1¾ oz) ricotta cheese
250 g (9 oz) packet round won ton or gow gee wrappers

To make the tomato sauce, heat the oil in a saucepan and cook the onion and garlic for 2–3 minutes, then stir in the tomato paste, wine, stock and tomato and simmer for 20 minutes. Stir in the basil.

To make the ravioli, combine the chicken, basil, parmesan, spring onion, ricotta and some salt and pepper. Lay 24 of the won ton wrappers on a flat surface and brush with a little water. Place slightly heaped teaspoons of the mixture onto the centre of each wrapper. Place another wrapper on top and press the edges together.

Bring a large saucepan of salted water to the boil. Add the ravioli, a few at a time, and cook for 2–3 minutes, or until just tender. Drain well and serve with the tomato sauce.

SERVES 4

Far left: For the tomato sauce, add the basil to the tomato mixture.

Left: Place the mixture between two wrappers and press together to make the ravioli.

Chapter 6

BAKED PASTA

Sheets of pasta layered with ragù or rich tomato sauce and a smooth, creamy béchamel, then finished with grated parmesan and left in the oven to bubble and melt until the smell becomes irresistible... Lasagne is undoubtedly the most famous baked pasta dish of our times, but there are many other tempting baked pasta recipes to enjoy.

Lasagne Classiche
Classic Lasagne

250 g (9 oz) lasagne sheets
75 g (2½ oz/½ cup) grated mozzarella cheese
60 g (2¼ oz/½ cup) grated cheddar cheese
125 ml (4 fl oz/½ cup) pouring (whipping) cream
3 tablespoons grated parmesan cheese

CHEESE SAUCE
60 g (2¼ oz) salted butter
40 g (1½ oz/⅓ cup) plain (all-purpose) flour
500 ml (17 fl oz/2 cups) milk
125 g (4½ oz/1 cup) grated cheddar cheese

MEAT SAUCE
1 tablespoon olive oil
1 onion, finely chopped
1 garlic clove, crushed
500 g (1 lb 2 oz) minced (ground) beef
850 g (1 lb 14 oz) tinned chopped tomatoes
3 tablespoons dry red wine
½ teaspoon ground oregano
¼ teaspoon ground basil

Preheat the oven to 180°C (350°F/Gas 4). Brush a shallow ovenproof dish approximately 24 x 30 cm (9½ x 12 inches) with melted butter or oil. Line with lasagne sheets, breaking them to fill any gaps, and set aside.

To make the cheese sauce, melt the butter in a saucepan. Add the flour and stir for 1 minute. Remove from the heat and slowly add the milk, stirring until smooth. Return to the heat and cook, stirring, over medium heat until the sauce boils and thickens. Reduce the heat and simmer for 3 minutes. Stir in the cheese, season and set aside.

To make the meat sauce, heat the oil in a large saucepan. Add the onion and garlic and stir over low heat until the onion is tender. Add the minced beef and brown well, breaking up with a wooden spoon as it cooks. Stir in the tomato, wine, oregano, basil and season. Bring to the boil, reduce the heat and simmer for 20 minutes.

Spoon one-third of the meat sauce over the lasagne sheets. Top with one-third of the cheese sauce. Arrange another layer of lasagne sheets over the top.

Continue layering, finishing with lasagne sheets. Sprinkle with the combined mozzarella and cheddar cheeses. Pour the cream over the top. Sprinkle with parmesan cheese. Bake for 35–40 minutes, or until golden.

SERVES 4–6

Right: Arrange a layer of lasagne sheets in the base of an ovenproof dish.

Far right: Spread a layer of meat sauce over the lasagne sheets and then build up the layers.

Pollo Veloce e Pasta al Forno
Speedy Chicken and Pasta bake

This recipe can also be made in a 2 litre (70 fl oz/8 cup) ovenproof dish and baked for 40 minutes, or until the cheese has melted.

200 g (7 oz) spiral pasta
425 g (15 oz) tinned cream of mushroom or
  broccoli soup
250 g (9 oz/1 cup) sour cream
1 teaspoon curry powder

1 barbecued chicken
250 g (9 oz) broccoli, cut into florets
90 g (3¼ oz/1 cup) fresh breadcrumbs
185 g (6½ oz/1½ cups) grated cheddar cheese

Preheat the oven to 180°C (350°F/Gas 4). Cook the pasta in a large saucepan of rapidly boiling salted water until al dente. Drain well and return to the pan to keep warm.

Combine the soup, sour cream and curry powder and season to taste with freshly ground black pepper.

Remove the meat from the chicken and roughly chop. Combine the chicken with the pasta, broccoli and soup mixture. Spoon into four lightly greased 500 ml (17 fl oz/2 cup) ovenproof dishes and sprinkle with the combined breadcrumbs and cheese. Bake for 25–30 minutes, or until the cheese melts.

SERVES 4

Far left: Mix together the soup, sour cream and curry powder to make the sauce.

Left: Mix together the chicken meat, pasta, broccoli and sauce.

Orzo e Formaggio Greco al Forno
Orzo and Greek Cheese Bake

Kefalotyri is a cheese normally made from sheep's milk. It is allowed to ripen for three months which gives it a sharp taste and a firm texture You can use romano if kefalotyri isn't readily available.

415 g (14¾ oz/2 cups) orzo
60 g (2¼ oz) salted butter
6 spring onions (scallions), chopped
450 g (1 lb) English spinach, chopped
2 tablespoons plain (all-purpose) flour

1.25 litres (44 fl oz/5 cups) milk
250 g (9 oz) kefalotyri cheese, grated
250 g (9 oz) marinated feta cheese, drained
3 tablespoons chopped dill

Preheat the oven to 190°C (375°F/Gas 5). Cook the pasta in a large saucepan of rapidly boiling salted water until al dente. Drain well and return to the pan keep warm. Heat 1 tablespoon of the butter in a large saucepan over high heat and cook the spring onion for 30 seconds. Add the spinach and stir for 1 minute, or until wilted. Season and stir into the pasta.

Put the remaining butter in the saucepan in which the spinach was cooked. Melt over low heat, then stir in the flour and cook for 1 minute, or until pale and foaming. Remove from the heat and gradually stir in the milk. Return to the heat and stir constantly for 5 minutes, or until the sauce boils and thickens. Add two-thirds of the kefalotyri and all of the feta and stir for 2 minutes until melted. Remove from the heat and stir in the dill.

Combine the pasta mixture with the cheese sauce, season to taste and pour into a lightly greased 2.5 litre (87 fl oz/10 cup) ovenproof dish. Sprinkle the remaining cheese on top and bake for 15 minutes, or until golden.

SERVES 4

Cook the spinach until wilted, then season well and stir into the orzo.

Cannelloni di Manzo e Spinaci
Beef and Spinach Cannelloni

You can use a piping bag to fill the cannelloni, but if you don't have one a teaspoon will do just as well.

FILLING
1 tablespoon olive oil
1 onion, chopped
1 garlic clove, crushed
500 g (1 lb 2 oz) minced (ground) beef
250 g (9 oz) frozen spinach, thawed
3 tablespoons tomato paste (concentrated purée)
125 g (4½ oz/½ cup) ricotta cheese
1 egg
½ teaspoon ground oregano

BECHAMEL SAUCE
250 ml (9 fl oz/1 cup) milk
1 parsley sprig
5 peppercorns
30 g (1 oz) salted butter
1 tablespoon plain (all-purpose) flour
125 ml (4 fl oz/½ cup) pouring (whipping) cream

TOMATO SAUCE
425 g (15 oz) tin tomato passata
   (puréed tomato)
2 tablespoons chopped basil
1 garlic clove, crushed
½ teaspoon sugar

12–15 instant cannelloni tubes
150 g (5½ oz/1 cup) grated mozzarella cheese
60 g (2¼ oz/½ cup) grated parmesan cheese

Preheat the oven to 180°C (350°F/Gas 4).
To make the filling, heat the oil in a frying pan. Add the onion and garlic; stir over low heat until onion is tender. Add the beef and brown well. Add spinach and tomato paste. Cook, stirring, for 1 minute. Remove from the heat. Mix the ricotta, egg and oregano. Stir into the beef mixture.

To make the béchamel sauce, put the milk, parsley and peppercorns in a small saucepan. Bring to the boil. Remove from heat and cool for 10 minutes. Strain, discarding the flavourings. Melt the butter in a small saucepan and stir in the flour. Cook, stirring, for 1 minute. Remove from the heat. Gradually stir in the strained milk until smooth.

Return to the heat and stir constantly over medium heat until the sauce boils and thickens. Reduce heat and simmer for 3 minutes. Add cream and season.

To make the tomato sauce, put all the ingredients in a pan and bring to the boil. Reduce the heat and simmer for 5 minutes. Pipe the filling into cannelloni tubes. Spoon a little of the tomato sauce in the base of a large ovenproof dish. Arrange the cannelloni on top. Pour béchamel sauce over the cannelloni, followed by the remaining tomato sauce. Sprinkle the cheeses over the top. Bake for 30–35 minutes, or until golden.

SERVES 4–6

Frittata di Spaghetti al Forno
Baked Spaghetti Frittata

30 g (1 oz) salted butter
125 g (4½ oz) button mushrooms, sliced
1 red or green capsicum (pepper), seeded and chopped
125 g (4½ oz) ham, sliced
90 g (3¼ oz/½ cup) frozen peas

6 eggs
250 ml (9 fl oz/1 cup) pouring (whipping) cream or milk
100 g (3½ oz) cooked spaghetti, chopped
2 tablespoons chopped parsley
3 tablespoons grated parmesan cheese

Preheat the oven to 180°C (350°F/Gas 4). Grease a 23 cm (9 inch) round ovenproof dish. Melt the butter in a frying pan and add the mushrooms. Cook over low heat for 2–3 minutes. Add the capsicum and cook for 1 minute. Stir in the ham and peas. Remove from the heat to cool.

Whisk together the eggs and cream and season. Add the spaghetti, parsley and mushroom mixture and stir. Pour into the dish and sprinkle with parmesan cheese. Bake for 25–30 minutes.

PICTURE ON OPPOSITE PAGE

SERVES 4

Maccheroni al Formaggio
Macaroni Cheese

225 g (8 oz) macaroni
90 g (3¼ oz) salted butter
1 onion, finely chopped
3 tablespoons plain (all-purpose) flour
500 ml (17 fl oz/2 cups) milk

2 teaspoons wholegrain mustard
150 g (5½ oz) mature cheddar cheese, grated
100 g (3½ oz) cheddar cheese, grated
30 g (1 oz) fresh breadcrumbs

Cook the pasta. Drain well and return to the pan to keep warm.

Preheat the oven to 180°C (350°F/Gas 4). Grease a 1.5 litre (52 fl oz/6 cup) ovenproof dish.

Melt the butter in a large saucepan over low heat, add the onion and cook for 5 minutes, or until softened. Stir in the flour and cook for 1 minute, or until pale and foaming. Remove from the heat and gradually stir in the milk. Return to

the heat and stir constantly until the sauce boils and thickens. Reduce the heat and simmer for 2 minutes. Stir in the mustard and about three-quarters of the combined cheeses. Season to taste. Add the cooked pasta to the pan and stir until coated in the mixture. Spoon into the dish and smooth the surface.

Combine the breadcrumbs and remaining cheese and scatter over the top. Bake for about 15 minutes, or until golden brown and bubbling.

SERVES 4

Pasta ai Frutti di Mare al Forno
Baked Seafood Pasta

This comforting family bake takes under 15 minutes to prepare and will be on the table in less than 45 minutes.

250 g (9 oz) lasagne sheets
500 g (1 lb 2 oz) boneless fish fillets
125 g (4½ oz) scallops
500 g (1 lb 2 oz) raw prawns (shrimp), peeled and
   deveined
125 g (4½ oz) salted butter
1 leek, sliced

90 g (3¼ oz/¾ cup) plain (all-purpose) flour
500 ml (17 fl oz/2 cups) milk
500 ml (17 fl oz/2 cups) dry white wine
125 g (4½ oz/1 cup) grated cheddar cheese
125 ml (4 fl oz/½ cup) pouring (whipping) cream
60 g (2¼ oz) grated parmesan cheese
2 tablespoons chopped parsley

Preheat the oven to 180°C (350°F/Gas 4). Grease a shallow 24 x 30 cm (9½ x 12 inch) ovenproof dish and line with lasagne sheets, breaking them to fill any gaps. Chop the fish and scallops into bite-sized pieces. Chop the prawns.

Melt the butter in a large saucepan and cook the leek, stirring, for 1 minute. Add the flour and cook, stirring, for 1 minute. Remove from the heat and slowly stir in the milk and wine until smooth. Return to medium heat and stir constantly until the sauce boils and thickens. Reduce the heat and simmer for 3 minutes. Stir in the cheddar cheese and seafood, season and simmer for 1 minute.

Spoon half the seafood sauce over the lasagne sheets. Top with another layer of lasagne sheets. Continue layering the sauce and the sheets, finishing with lasagne sheets.

Pour the cream over the top. Sprinkle with the combined parmesan and parsley and bake for 30 minutes, or until bubbling and golden.

SERVES 4–6

Right: Cut the fish and scallops into bite-sized pieces and chop the prawns.

Far right: Slowly stir in the wine and milk and stir until the sauce is smooth.

Cannelloni ai Frutti di Mare
Seafood Cannelloni

You can vary the seafood used in this recipe according to your preference or what is in season. Use a teaspoon to stuff the mixture into the tubes.

FILLING
1 onion, sliced
1 carrot, sliced
1 celery stalk, cut in half
1 bouquet garni
250 ml (9 fl oz/1 cup) dry white wine
4 whole black peppercorns
300 g (10½ oz) scallops
500 g (1 lb 2 oz) raw prawns (shrimp), peeled and
    deveined
300 g (10½ oz) skinless fish fillets (such as flathead,
    flake, hake, ling, cod), boned and chopped
60 g (2¼ oz) salted butter

1 onion, finely chopped
200 g (7 oz) button mushrooms, finely chopped
800 g (1 lb 12 oz) tinned chopped tomatoes
2 tablespoons chopped parsley
2 tablespoons chopped basil
2 tablespoons pouring (whipping) cream
15 cannelloni tubes
125 g (4½ oz) grated cheddar cheese

BECHAMEL SAUCE
60 g (2¼ oz) salted butter
2 tablespoons plain (all-purpose) flour
750 ml (26 fl oz/3 cups) milk

Preheat the oven to 180°C (350°F/Gas 4). Combine the onion, carrot, celery, bouquet garni and 500 ml (17 fl oz/2 cups) water in a large saucepan and bring to the boil. Reduce the heat and simmer for 15 minutes. Add the wine and peppercorns and simmer for 15 minutes. Strain, discard the vegetables and reserve the liquid.

Cut the seafood small enough to enable it to fit in the cannelloni tubes.

Put the reserved liquid in a clean saucepan. Bring to the boil. Add the seafood. Reduce the heat and simmer until tender. Strain and reserve the liquid.

Melt the butter in a large frying pan, add the onion and cook until golden brown. Add the mushrooms and cook until tender. Add 3 tablespoons of the reserved liquid, tomato and herbs; bring to the boil. Reduce the heat; simmer for 30 minutes, or until the sauce thickens. Stir in the seafood and cream. Season.

To make the sauce, melt butter in a saucepan, add flour; stir for 1 minute, or until pale and foaming. Remove from the heat and gradually stir in milk. Return to heat and stir until the sauce comes to the boil and thickens.

Spoon the mixture into the cannelloni tubes. Place in a greased 3 litre (105 fl oz/12 cup) ovenproof dish. Pour the sauce over and sprinkle with grated cheese. Bake for 40 minutes, or until cannelloni tubes are tender.

SERVES 6

PASTICCIO

Pastitsio

Kefalotyri and manchego are firm, grating cheeses from Greece and Spain respectively. You can use parmesan instead if they aren't readily available.

2 tablespoons olive oil
4 garlic cloves, crushed
3 onions, chopped
1 kg (2 lb 4 oz) minced (ground) lamb
800 g (1 lb 12 oz) tinned chopped tomatoes
250 ml (9 fl oz/1 cup) dry red wine
250 ml (9 fl oz/1 cup) chicken stock
3 tablespoons tomato paste (concentrated purée)
2 tablespoons oregano leaves

2 bay leaves
350 g (12 oz) ziti or spaghetti
2 eggs, lightly beaten
750 g (1 lb 10 oz/3 cups) Greek-style yoghurt
3 eggs, extra, lightly beaten
200 g (7 oz) kefalotyri or manchego cheese, grated
½ teaspoon ground nutmeg
50 g (1¾ oz/½ cup) grated parmesan cheese
80 g (2¾ oz/1 cup) fresh breadcrumbs

Preheat the oven to 200°C (400°F/Gas 6). To make the meat sauce, heat the oil in a large heavy-based saucepan and cook the garlic and onion over low heat for 10 minutes, or until the onion is soft and golden.

Add the lamb and cook over high heat until browned, stirring constantly and breaking up any lumps with a wooden spoon. Add the tomato, wine, stock, tomato paste, oregano and bay leaves. Bring to the boil, reduce the heat and simmer, covered, for 15 minutes. Remove the lid and cook for 30 minutes. Season with salt and pepper.

While the meat is cooking, cook the pasta in a large saucepan of rapidly boiling salted water until al dente. Drain well. Transfer to a bowl and stir the eggs through. Spoon into a lightly greased 4 litre (140 fl oz/16 cup) ovenproof dish. Top with the meat sauce.

Whisk the yoghurt, extra eggs, cheese and nutmeg in a bowl to combine and pour the mixture over the meat sauce. Sprinkle with the combined parmesan cheese and breadcrumbs. Bake for 30–35 minutes, or until the top of the pastitsio is crisp and golden. Leave for 20 minutes before slicing.

SERVES 8

Far left: Cook the minced lamb until browned before adding the tomato, wine, stock, tomato paste and herbs.

Left: Pour the mixture of yoghurt, eggs, cheese and nutmeg over the meat sauce.

Conchiglie ripiene di Ricotta con Sugo di Pollo
Ricotta-stuffed Pasta Shells with Chicken Sauce

Filled pasta freezes well and must be cooked straight from the freezer, not defrosted. To freeze filled pasta, do so in a single layer or, if necessary, between sheets of baking paper. Cover with a tea towel. When frozen, transfer to an airtight container.

500 g (1 lb 2 oz) conchiglie (large pasta shells)
2 tablespoons olive oil
1 onion, chopped
1 garlic clove, crushed
60 g (2¼ oz) prosciutto, sliced
125 g (4½ oz) button mushrooms, chopped
250 g (9 oz) minced (ground) chicken
2 tablespoons tomato paste (concentrated purée)

425 g (15 oz) tin chopped tomatoes
125 ml (4 fl oz/½ cup) dry white wine
1 teaspoon dried oregano
250 g (9 oz/1 cup) ricotta cheese
220 g (7¾ oz) mozzarella cheese, grated
1 teaspoon snipped chives
1 tablespoon chopped parsley
3 tablespoons grated parmesan cheese

Cook the pasta in a large saucepan of rapidly boiling salted water until al dente. Drain well and return to the pan to keep warm.

Meanwhile, heat the oil in a large frying pan. Add the onion and garlic, then stir over low heat until the onion is tender. Add the prosciutto and stir for 1 minute. Add the mushrooms and cook for 2 minutes. Add the chicken and brown well, breaking up any lumps with a fork as it cooks.

Stir in the tomato paste, tomato, wine and oregano and season to taste. Bring to the boil, reduce the heat and simmer for 20 minutes.

Preheat the oven to 180°C (350°F/Gas 4). Combine the ricotta, mozzarella, chives, parsley and half the parmesan cheese. Spoon a little into each shell. Spoon some of the chicken sauce into the base of an ovenproof dish. Arrange the conchiglie on top. Spread the remaining sauce over the top and sprinkle with the remaining parmesan. Bake 25–30 minutes, or until golden.

SERVES 4

Far left: Add the sliced prosciutto to the onion and garlic in a large frying pan.

Left: Carefully spoon some filling into each of the shells and then arrange in the dish.

Chapter 7

Soups and Salads

∗∗∗∗∗∗∗∗∗∗∗∗∗∗∗∗∗∗∗∗∗∗∗∗∗∗∗∗∗∗∗∗∗∗∗∗∗∗

The combination of fresh vegetables, finest-quality olive oil and cold al dente pasta has a distinct Mediterranean flavour. Few foods are so adaptable that they are delicious when served either hot or cold.

Zuppa di Fagioli con Salsiccia
Bean Soup with Sausage

Rather than using tinned beans you can use dried beans which have been soaked overnight. Make sure that they are drained before adding to the soup (see note below).

2 teaspoons olive oil
4 Italian sausages, diced
2 leeks, sliced
1 garlic clove, crushed
1 large carrot, finely diced
2 celery stalks, sliced
2 tablespoons plain (all-purpose) flour

2 beef stock (bouillon) cubes, crumbled
125 ml (4 fl oz/½ cup) dry white wine
125 g (4½ oz) small pasta shells
440 g (15½ oz) tinned three-bean mix, drained and
rinsed
1 teaspoon chopped chilli (optional)

Heat the oil in a large heavy-based saucepan and add the sausage. Cook over medium heat for 5 minutes or until golden, stirring regularly. Drain on paper towels.

Add the leek, garlic, carrot and celery to the pan and cook, stirring occasionally, for 2–3 minutes or until soft.

Add the flour and cook, stirring, for 1 minute. Add the stock cubes and wine and gradually stir in 2 litres (70 fl oz/8 cups) water. Bring to the boil, then reduce the heat and simmer for 10 minutes.

Add the pasta, beans and chilli (if using) to the pan. Increase the heat and cook for 8–10 minutes, or until the pasta is al dente. Return the sausage to the saucepan and season to taste.

Note: Use dried beans, if preferred. Place in a bowl; cover with water; soak overnight. Drain; add to a large saucepan with water to come about 3 cm (1¼ inches) above the beans; simmer for 1 hour. Drain well before adding to the soup.

SERVES 4–6

Far left: Add the leek, garlic, carrot and celery and cook, stirring occasionally, until soft.

Left: Add the stock and then the wine and water and bring to the boil.

ZUPPA DI POLLO E VERDURE
Chicken and Vegetable soup

750 g (1 lb 10 oz) pumpkin (winter squash)
2 all-purpose potatoes
1 tablespoon olive oil
30 g (1 oz) salted butter
1 large onion, finely chopped

2 garlic cloves, crushed
3 litres (105 fl oz/12 cups) chicken stock
125 g (4½ oz) miniature pasta or risoni
1 tablespoon chopped parsley, for serving

Peel the pumpkin and potatoes and chop into small cubes. Heat the oil and butter in a large saucepan. Add the onion and garlic and cook, stirring, for 5 minutes over low heat.

Add the pumpkin, potato and chicken stock. Increase the heat, cover and cook for 8 minutes, or until the vegetables are tender.

Add the pasta and cook, stirring occasionally, for 5 minutes or until the pasta is al dente. Serve immediately, sprinkled with the chopped parsley.

Notes: Butternut or jap (kent) pumpkin will give this soup the sweetest flavour.

Tiny star-shaped pasta look attractive in this soup.

PICTURE ON OPPOSITE PAGE

SERVES 4

ZUCCA CAMPAGNOLA E ZUPPA DI PASTA
Country Pumpkin and Pasta Soup

1 tablespoon oil
1 carrot, sliced
1 leek, chopped
2 boneless, skinless chicken thighs, cut into
  bite-sized pieces

35 g (1¼ oz/¼ cup) ditalini or other small pasta
1 litre (35 fl oz/4 cups) vegetable stock
2 ripe tomatoes, diced

Heat the oil in a saucepan and cook the carrot and leek over medium heat for 4 minutes, or until soft. Add the chicken and cook for a further 2 minutes, or until the chicken has changed colour.

Add the pasta and the vegetable stock, cover and bring to the boil. Reduce the heat and simmer

for 10 minutes, or until the pasta is cooked. Add the tomato halfway through the cooking. Season to taste with salt and pepper. Serve with fresh crusty bread.

SERVES 4–6

Zuppa di Ditalini al Pomodoro
Tomato Ditalini Soup

Ditalini, which means 'little thimbles' in Italian, is widely used in the Campania region of Italy, where it is a key component of many soups.

2 teaspoons olive oil
1 onion, chopped
1 carrot, chopped
2 celery stalks, chopped
350 g (12 oz) sweet potato, chopped

400 g (14 oz) tinned corn kernels, drained
1 litre (35 fl oz/4 cups) vegetable stock
90 g (3¼ oz/1 cup) ditalini pasta

Heat the oil in a large saucepan and add the onion, carrot and celery. Cook over low heat, stirring regularly, for 10 minutes, or until soft.

Add the sweet potato, corn kernels and stock.

Bring to the boil, reduce the heat and simmer for 20 minutes, or until the vegetables are tender. Add the pasta to the pan and return to the boil. Reduce the heat and simmer for 10 minutes, or until the pasta is al dente. Serve immediately.

PICTURE ON OPPOSITE PAGE   SERVES 4

Zuppa di Verdure Semplici e Pasta
Simple Vegetable and Pasta Soup

2 tablespoons olive oil
1 large onion, finely chopped
2 celery stalks, finely chopped
3 vine-ripened tomatoes

1.5 litres (52 fl oz/6 cups) chicken or vegetable stock
90 g (3¼ oz/½ cup) ditalini
2 tablespoons chopped parsley

Heat the oil in a large saucepan over medium heat. Add the onion and celery and cook for 5 minutes, or until they have softened.

Score a cross in the base of each tomato, then place in a bowl of boiling water for 1 minute. Plunge the tomatoes into cold water and peel the skin away from the cross. Halve the tomatoes and scoop out the seeds with a teaspoon. Roughly chop the flesh.

Add the stock and tomato to the pan and bring to the boil. Add the pasta and cook for 10 minutes, or until al dente. Season and sprinkle with parsley. Serve with crusty bread.

                                                                 SERVES 6

ZUPPA DI PASTA E FAGIOLI BIANCHI
Pasta and White Bean Soup

Cannellini beans are small, white and slightly kidney-shaped; they are widely used in Italian cooking, particularly in Tuscany.

PESTO
50 g (1¾ oz/⅓ cup) pine nuts
2 large handfuls basil leaves
50 g (1¾ oz) rocket (arugula) leaves
2 garlic cloves, chopped
35 g (1¼ oz/⅓ cup) finely grated parmesan cheese
4 tablespoons olive oil

185 g (6½ oz) spiral pasta
1.5 litres (52 fl oz/6 cups) chicken stock
600 g (1 lb 5 oz) tinned cannellini beans, drained
    and rinsed

Put the pine nuts in a dry frying pan and toast them over medium heat for 1–2 minutes, or until golden brown. Remove from the pan and allow to cool.

To make the pesto, mix the pine nuts, basil, rocket, garlic and parmesan in a food processor and process until finely chopped. With the motor running, add the oil in a thin stream until well combined. Season to taste with salt and pepper. Set aside.

Cook the pasta in rapidly boiling salted water until al dente. Heat the chicken stock in a large saucepan until it begins to boil. Reduce the heat to simmering point. Drain the pasta and add to the stock with the cannellini beans. Reheat and serve with a spoonful of pesto.

SERVES 6

Far left: Dry-fry the pine nuts until golden brown, but take care not to let them burn.

Left: Put the pine nuts, basil, rocket, garlic and parmesan cheese in a food processor.

Pesto Caldo e Insalata di Gamberi
Warm Pesto and Prawn Salad

You can make the pesto 2–3 months ahead (5–6 months ahead if kept frozen) as long as you omit the cheese. Stir through the cheese when the sauce is ready to be used.

PESTO
2 garlic cloves, crushed
1 teaspoon salt
40 g (1½ oz/¼ cup) pine nuts, toasted
2 very large handfuls basil
60 g (2¼ oz) grated parmesan cheese
3 tablespoons extra virgin olive oil

500 g (1 lb 2 oz) pasta
150 g (5½ oz) jar capers in brine

3 tablespoons olive oil
2 tablespoons extra virgin olive oil
2 garlic cloves, chopped
2 tomatoes, seeded and diced
150 g (5½ oz) asparagus spears trimmed, halved and blanched
2 tablespoons balsamic vinegar
150 g (5½ oz) rocket (arugula)
20 cooked prawns (shrimp), peeled, tails intact
shaved parmesan cheese, for serving

For the pesto, blend the garlic, salt, pine nuts, basil leaves and parmesan cheese in a food processor or blender until thoroughly combined. With the motor running, add the oil in a thin steady stream and process until the pesto is smooth.

Cook the pasta in a large saucepan of rapidly boiling salted water until al dente. Drain well, transfer to a large bowl and toss the pesto through.

Pat the drained capers dry with paper towels, then heat the olive oil in a frying pan and fry the capers for 4–5 minutes, stirring occasionally, until crisp.

Drain on paper towels.

Heat the extra virgin olive oil in a deep frying pan over medium heat and add the garlic, tomato and asparagus. Toss continuously for 1–2 minutes, or until warmed through. Stir in the balsamic vinegar.

When the pasta is just warm, not hot (or it will wilt the rocket), toss the tomato mixture, rocket and prawns through it and season with salt and pepper, to taste. Serve sprinkled with capers and shaved parmesan (if desired).

SERVES 4

Insalata di Pasta e Salame
Salami Pasta Salad

1 red capsicum (pepper), cut into strips
1 green capsicum (pepper), cut into strips
4 celery stalks, sliced
1 fennel bulb, trimmed and sliced
1 red onion, sliced
200 g (7 oz) salami, thickly sliced and then cut into strips
1 large handful chopped flat-leaf (Italian) parsley
300 g (10½ oz) fettuccine

DRESSING
125 ml (4 fl oz/½ cup) olive oil
3 tablespoons lemon juice
2½ tablespoons dijon mustard
1 teaspoon sugar
1 garlic clove, crushed

Mix together the capsicum, celery, fennel, onion, salami and parsley in a large bowl.

Cook the pasta in a large saucepan of rapidly boiling salted water until al dente. Drain well and rinse under cold water. Add to the bowl and toss with the vegetables and salami.

To make the dressing, combine the olive oil, lemon juice, mustard, sugar and crushed garlic and season to taste. Pour over the pasta salad and toss well.

PICTURE ON OPPOSITE PAGE

SERVES 8

Peperone Grigliato e Insalata d'Acciughe
Grilled Capsicum and Anchovy Salad

500 g (1 lb 2 oz) penne or spiral pasta
2 large red capsicums (peppers)
1 small red onion, finely chopped
2 large handfuls flat-leaf (Italian) parsley

2 anchovies, whole or chopped
3 tablespoons olive oil
2 tablespoons lemon juice

Cook the pasta in a large saucepan of rapidly boiling salted water until al dente. Drain and rinse under cold water.

Cut the capsicum into large pieces, removing the seeds and membrane. Place skin side up under a hot grill (broiler) and cook for 8 minutes, or until

the skin is blistered and black. Cool in a plastic bag, then peel away the skin and cut the flesh into thin strips.

Toss together the pasta, capsicum, onion, parsley, anchovies, oil, lemon juice and season. Serve immediately.

SERVES 4–6

Insalata di Pasta Mediterranea con Olive Nere
Mediterranean Pasta Salad with Black Olive Dressing

250 g (9 oz) spiral pasta
1 red capsicum (pepper)
1 yellow or green capsicum (pepper)
1 tablespoon sunflower oil
2 tablespoons olive oil
2 garlic cloves, crushed
1 eggplant (aubergine), cubed
2 zucchini (courgettes), thickly sliced
2 large ripe tomatoes, peeled, seeded and chopped

1 handful chopped flat-leaf (Italian) parsley
150 g (5½ oz/1 cup) crumbled feta cheese

BLACK OLIVE DRESSING
6 large marinated black olives, pitted
125 ml (4 fl oz/½ cup) olive oil
2 tablespoons balsamic vinegar

Cook the pasta in a large saucepan of rapidly boiling salted water until al dente. Drain well, spread in a single layer on a baking tray to dry, then refrigerate, uncovered, until chilled.

Cut the capsicum into large pieces, removing the seeds and membrane. Place, skin side up, under a hot grill (broiler) until the skin blackens and blisters. Leave to cool in a plastic bag, then peel away the skin. Slice the flesh into thick strips.

Heat the sunflower and olive oil in a frying pan. Add the garlic and eggplant and fry quickly, tossing, until lightly browned. Remove from the heat and place in a large bowl. Steam the zucchini for 1–2 minutes, or until just tender. Rinse under cold water, drain and add to the eggplant.

To make the dressing, process the olives in a food processor until finely chopped. Gradually add the olive oil, processing until thoroughly combined after each addition. Add the vinegar, season and process to combine.

Combine the pasta, capsicum, eggplant, zucchini, tomato, parsley and 1 teaspoon pepper in a large bowl. Top with the feta and drizzle with the dressing.

Note: To peel tomatoes, score a cross in the base of each tomato. Leave in a pan of boiling water for 1 minute, then plunge into cold water. Peel the skin away from the cross. To remove the seeds, cut the tomato in half and scoop out the seeds with a teaspoon.

SERVES 4

Far left: Drain the cooked pasta and spread on a tray to dry and cool.

Left: Remove the seeds and white membrane from the capsicums and cut into large pieces.

Insalata di Manzo e Pesto
Pesto Beef Salad

Don't wash the mushrooms as the water penetrates the delicate flesh and makes them soggy. Instead, wipe them gently with a damp cloth or paper towel.

100 g (3½ oz) button mushrooms
1 large yellow capsicum (pepper)
1 large red capsicum (pepper)
cooking oil spray
100 g (3½ oz) lean fillet steak
125 g (4½ oz/1½ cups) penne

PESTO
2 large handfuls basil leaves
2 garlic cloves, chopped
2 tablespoons pepitas (pumpkin seeds)
1 tablespoon olive oil
2 tablespoons orange juice
1 tablespoon lemon juice

Cut the mushrooms into quarters. Cut the capsicums into quarters, discarding the seeds and membrane. Grill (broil) the capsicum, skin side up, until the skins blacken and blister. Cool under a damp tea towel (dish towel), then peel and dice the flesh.

Spray a non-stick frying pan with oil and cook the steak over high heat for 3–4 minutes on each side. Remove and leave for 5 minutes before cutting into thin slices. Season with a little salt.

To make the pesto, finely chop the basil leaves, garlic and pepitas in a food processor. With the motor running, add the oil, orange and lemon juice. Season well.

Meanwhile, cook the pasta in a large saucepan of rapidly boiling salted water until al dente. Drain well and toss with the pesto in a large bowl.

Add the capsicum pieces, steak slices and mushroom quarters to the penne and toss to distribute evenly. Serve immediately.

SERVES 4

Add the oil as well as the orange and lemon juice in a thin stream.

Basics

An important step in mastering any cuisine is learning
the basic recipes and techniques. Straight from the recipe journal,
here are the ones no pasta cook should be without.

Impasto per Pasta Base
Basic Pasta Dough

When making pasta dough, use '00' flour, a very finely ground flour with a high gluten content, which helps with the structure of the pasta. Kneading adds strength to the pasta so that it holds up well during cooking. Resting is also essential, as it reduces the chance of shrinkage as you roll and cook the pasta. This quantity will serve four as a main and eight as a starter.

375 g (13 oz/2½ cups) '00' flour, plus extra 1 teaspoon salt

3 eggs, at room temperature

3-4 egg yolks, at room temperature

3 teaspoons olive oil

Sift the flour and salt together onto a clean work surface and make a well in the centre.

Crack the eggs into a measuring jug. Add the yolks one at a time—you require 220 ml (7½ fl oz) of egg and egg yolk in total (you may not need all of the yolks). Measuring ensures accuracy and helps if you are using organic eggs, which are often different sizes.

Measure the olive oil. Pour the eggs and the olive oil into the well in the flour. Use the fingertips of one hand to break up the yolks, then move your fingers in a circular motion, gradually incorporating the flour. Then use both hands to bring it together into a rough dough.

Knead for 8 minutes or until the dough is smooth and elastic. Divide the dough into two equal portions, shape into balls and cover with a slightly damp cloth.

Spinach pasta: Blanch 250 g (9 oz) trimmed English spinach leaves in boiling water until just wilted and bright green. Drain and refresh under cold running water. Use your hands and then a cloth to squeeze out any excess water. Then use a food processor to finely chop the spinach. Add to the flour with the eggs. As you knead the dough the spinach will be speckled throughout it. Once it has rested and you roll the dough, the rolling process will distribute the spinach evenly through the pasta.

Herb pasta: Add 2 tablespoons freshly chopped flat-leaf (Italian) parsley to the flour with the eggs.

Tomato pasta: Add ½ tablespoon tomato paste (concentrated purée) to the flour with the eggs; you may need to dust the pasta with flour as you knead, as it adds extra moisture, which can make the dough sticky.

Saffron pasta: Finely chop 1 teaspoon saffron threads and add to the flour with the eggs.

Chilli pasta: Add 1 teaspoon dried chilli flakes to the flour with the eggs.

Lemon and black pepper pasta: Add the finely grated zest of 2 lemons and ¼ teaspoon freshly ground black pepper (not too coarse, otherwise it will interfere with rolling) to the flour with the eggs.

Black pepper pasta: Add 1 teaspoon freshly ground black pepper (not too coarse, otherwise it will interfere with rolling) to the flour with the eggs.

MAKES 600 G (1 LB 6 OZ)

Stendere l'Impasto per Pasta Fresca
Rolling Fresh Pasta Dough

Plan ahead by deciding which shape you are going to cut and by ensuring that you have a large enough work surface for the sheets.

Set a pasta machine on the thickest setting. (It is a good idea to attach the cutter attachment to the pasta machine even when just rolling sheets of pasta—it helps to support the pasta.) Dust one portion of the dough very lightly with flour, then use a rolling pin to roll out to the thickness of the widest setting of your pasta machine. Keep the other ball of dough covered with a slightly damp cloth until needed.

Feed the dough into the rollers. Use one hand to turn the handle and the other hand to support the dough as it comes through the roller. If the pasta doesn't come through evenly, fold it into thirds, turn it 90 degrees and pass it through again.

Pass the dough through the machine one or two more times until about 70 cm (28 inches) long, lightly dusting with flour if necessary and reducing the roller setting by one notch after each rolling. This process both rolls the pasta into sheets and works the gluten in the wheat to give the pasta a firm, strong texture.

Return the machine to the thickest setting. Fold the dough back on itself in half and pass it, open end first, through the machine. Then pass the dough through one or two more times, reducing the roller setting by one notch each time. When the pasta is about 80 cm (32 inches) long, cut it in half widthways. Lay one portion of dough flat on the work surface and cover with a slightly damp cloth while you continue working with the other half.

Return the machine to the thickest setting. Fold one half of the pasta into thirds and use a rolling pin to roll it out to the thickness of the widest setting of your pasta machine. Keep in mind not to roll the piece too wide—it should be about 1 cm (½ inch) less than the width of your rollers as you want the finished sheet to gradually get wider as you roll. This is important for making ravioli and other filled pastas.

Pass the dough, open end first, through the rollers. (Turning the dough and passing it through the rollers at a different angle gives strength and elasticity to the pasta.)

Continue to pass the dough through the pasta machine, dusting lightly with flour as necessary and reducing the roller setting by one notch after each rolling, until less than 1 mm (1/32 inch) thick, (or to the thickness required in your recipe). You may need to cut the pasta in half at some point, depending on how much bench space you have and how easy you find the pasta to handle.

When the rolling is completed, the pasta should be so thin that you can see the shadow of an open fingered hand underneath.

Once you have completed the rolling process, the pasta is ready for cutting or filling. (If you're going to use the sheets for filled pasta, don't dust them with any more flour at this stage, as that will prevent the sheets from sticking together once filled.)

Repeat the rolling and cutting or filling with the other half of the dough.

Tagliare l'Impasto per Pasta Fresca
Cutting Fresh Pasta Dough

Cutting by either method will become much easier with practice.

CUTTING BY MACHINE

Most pasta machines come with an attachment that cuts ribbon pastas. You should attach this when rolling as it helps to support the pasta as you feed it through.

Dust the rolled-out pasta sheets quite generously with flour on both sides, and begin to feed them through the machine.

As the strands emerge, catch them on your hand to gently support them. Discard the outer strands from cutting, as they are often uneven.

Either hang the pasta up to dry completely or coil it into nests.

CUTTING BY HAND

Only ribbon pastas can be cut by hand—shapes, such as spaghetti, need to be done by machine.

Don't get too carried away with neatness; a rustic look is appropriate for handcut. Dust a pasta sheet quite generously with flour on both sides, then cut into desired lengths. Fold several times to form a loose roll (or roll around a rolling pin), keeping the sides straight as you fold.

Use a large sharp knife to cut as desired: 8 mm (⅜ inch) thick for fettuccine or 2 cm (¾ inch) thick for pappardelle.

Carefully unravel the pasta and dry.

Asciugare l'Impasto per Pasta Fresca
Drying Fresh Pasta Dough

You can buy pasta drying racks, but it's easy enough to improvise your own, for example by hanging ribbons of cut pasta over a clean broom handle suspended between two chairs. A clothes-drying rack also works well.

Set up your pasta drying rack, then hang the cut pasta over it.

Some pastas, such as fettuccine, can be hung to dry for an hour or so, then rolled into small nests while still pliable. This makes the pasta less likely to break during storage.

Place the nests on the base of a large, lightly floured airtight container and leave for 24 hours (with the lid off) to dry completely.

Seal the container and store in a cool place for up to 1 week. You could also use a large, deep-sided tray and wrap it well in plastic wrap so it is airtight.

Note. If you are making pasta to cook immediately, you can roll it out, hang it to partially dry, prepare your sauce and then cook the pasta just before you're ready to serve. Any leftover pasta should be dried completely and stored as described above.

Dare una forma alla Pasta Ripiena
Shaping Filled Pasta

After the final roll through the machine don't sprinkle the pasta with flour as you will need the sheets to stick together later.

RAVIOLI

Place one rolled pasta sheet on a very lightly floured surface. Keep other sheets covered. Place 1 teaspoon of filling on the pasta sheet, leaving 4 cm (1½ inches) between the mounds.

Brush around the filling lightly with some beaten egg. Place another pasta sheet on top, then press around the edge of the filling to enclose it, taking care to expel any air.

Cut into 6.5 cm (2½ inch) square ravioli using a fluted pastry wheel. Place, so they are not touching, in a single layer on a tray lined with lightly floured baking paper. Repeat with remaining dough and filling.

AGNOLOTTI

Place a pasta sheet on a lightly floured surface. Cut out 6.5 cm (2½ inch) rounds. Cover the cut rounds with a clean cloth so they don't dry out.

Place 1 teaspoon of filling in the centre of each round and brush the edges lightly with beaten egg.

Fold into a half moon, pressing the edges to seal and taking care to expel any air. Place in a single layer on a tray lined with lightly floured baking paper, ensuring the pasta edges aren't touching. Repeat with remaining dough and filling.

TORTELLINI

Place a pasta sheet on a lightly floured surface. Cut 6.5 cm (2½ inch) rounds from the pasta sheets. Cover with a clean cloth. Place ¼ teaspoon of filling in the centre of each round. Brush the edges with some beaten egg.

Fold into a half moon, pressing the edges to seal and expel any air. Wrap the folded side around your fingertip, brushing one edge lightly with beaten egg, and pinch to seal.

Place, so they are not touching, in a single layer on a tray lined with lightly floured baking paper.

Far left: Place the mixture between two wrappers and press together to make the ravioli...

Left: Wrap the semi-circles around your finger to make a ring and press the ends together to make the tortellini.

Besciamella
Béchamel Sauce

65 g (2¼ oz) butter
40 g (1½ oz) plain (all-purpose) flour
pinch of grated nutmeg

625 ml (21½ fl oz/2½ cups) milk
1 bay leaf

Heat the butter in a saucepan over low heat. Add the flour and nutmeg and cook, stirring, for 1 minute. Remove from the heat and gradually stir in the milk. Add the bay leaf, return to the heat and simmer, stirring often, until the sauce thickens. Season, cover with plastic wrap to prevent a skin forming, and cool. Discard the bay leaf.

MAKES 750 ML (26 FL OZ/3 CUPS)

Sugo al Pomodoro
Tomato Sauce

120 g (4 oz) plum (roma) tomatoes
3 basil leaves
2 garlic cloves, crushed

1 tablespoon tomato passata
2 teaspoons extra virgin olive oil

Core the tomatoes and purée in a food processor with the basil leaves (or chop the tomatoes and basil very finely and stir together). Stir in the garlic, passata and olive oil and season well. Leave for at least 30 minutes before serving to allow the flavours to blend.

MAKES 185 ML (6 FL OZ/¾ CUP)

Pesto
Pesto

2 garlic cloves
50 g (1¾ oz//⅓ cup) pine nuts
80 g (2¾ oz/1¼ cups) basil leaves

4 tablespoons grated parmesan
150 ml (5 fl oz) extra virgin olive oil

Put the garlic, pine nuts, basil and parmesan in a mortar and pestle or a food processor and pound or mix to a paste. Add the oil in a steady stream, mixing continuously. Add salt if necessary.

MAKES 185 ML (6 FL OZ/¾ CUP)

GLOSSARY

AL DENTE Meaning 'to the bite'. Pasta and risotto rice are cooked until they are al dente—the outside is tender but the centre still has a little resistance or 'bite'. Pasta cooked beyond this point becomes soggy.

CANNELLINI BEANS These are white, kidney-shaped beans, also known as Italian haricot beans. Available fresh, dried or tinned.

CAPERS The pickled flowers of the caper bush. Available preserved in brine, vinegar or salt. Should be rinsed and squeezed dry before use.

FLAT-LEAF PARSLEY Also known as Italian or continental parsley. Used as an ingredient rather than a garnish, unlike curly parsley.

GORGONZOLA A blue cheese, originally made in Gorgonzola in Lombardia but now produced in other regions as well. It melts well and is often used in sauces. If not available, use another full-fat blue cheese.

MARSALA A fortified wine from Marsala in Sicily that comes in varying degrees of dryness and sweetness. Don't use sweet Marsala in savoury dishes.

MOZZARELLA Originally, all mozzarella in Italy was made from the prized milk of water buffaloes, which gives a creamy, fragrant cheese. Most mozzarella is now made with cow's milk.

OLIVE Varieties are often named after the region they come from, such as Ligurian; their curing style, such as Sicilian; or their variety, such as Cerignola. Though green and black olives

have a different flavour, they can be used interchangeably unless the final colour is a factor.

OLIVE OIL Extra virgin and virgin olive oils are pressed without any heat or chemicals and are best used in simple uncooked dishes and for salads. Pure olive oil can be used for cooking or deep-frying. Different varieties of olives are grown all over Italy and the oil of each region has a distinctive taste. Tuscan oil tends to be full-bodied and peppery; Ligurian oil subtle; and Pugliese and Sicilian oils fruity and sharp.

PARMIGIANO REGGIANO (PARMESAN) Perhaps Italy's most famous cheese. Produced in the Parma/Reggio region of Italy. By law it can only contain milk, salt, and rennet.

PASSATA Meaning 'puréed', this most commonly refers to a smooth uncooked tomato pulp bought in tins or jars. It is best to buy passata without added herbs and flavourings.

PECORINO One of Italy's most popular cheeses, with virtually every region producing its own version. Made from sheep's milk and always by the same method, taste varies according to age.

PEPERONCINI The Italian name for chillies, these are popular in the cooking of the South, and are also served there as a condiment. The smallest are called diavolilli.

PORCINI The Italian name for a cep or boletus mushroom. Usually bought dried and reconstituted by soaking in boiling water, but available fresh in the spring and autumn.

INDEX

Published in 2016 by Murdoch Books, an imprint of Allen & Unwin

Murdoch Books Australia
83 Alexander Street
Crows Nest NSW 2065
Phone: +61 (0) 2 8425 0100
www.murdochbooks.com.au
info@murdochbooks.com.au

Murdoch Books UK
Erico House, 6th Floor
93–99 Upper Richmond Road
Putney, London SW15 2TG
Phone: +44 (0) 20 8785 5995
www.murdochbooks.co.uk
info@murdochbooks.co.uk

For Corporate Orders & Custom Publishing contact Noel Hammond,
National Business Development Manager, Murdoch Books Australia

Editor: Audra Barclay
Series Design Manager: Sarah Odgers
Design: Ice Cold Publishing
Photography: Alan Benson and Chris L. Jones
Food styling: Mary Harris
Food preparation: Joanne Glynn
Production Manager: Alex Gonzalez

A cataloguing-in-publication entry is available from the catalogue of
the National Library of Australia at nla.gov.au.

ISBN 978 1 743366585 Australia
ISBN 978 1 743366592 UK

A catalogue record for this book is available from the British Library.

Colour reproduction by Splitting Image, Clayton, Victoria.
Printed by 1010 Printing International Limited, China.